'Here is distilled Ma[...]
ing, and writing, und[...]
stances, reduced to its [...]
cal malt flows, howe[...]
rather through the hear of Scottish theology. With headwaters in
the towering truths of Scripture, Macleod's résumé of the incarnation and atonement runs deep through Patristic and Reformation
teaching, gaining a force in the Modern period which is ignored to
one's intellectual peril. Though stripped of all notes and academic
vignettes, he deals with all the usual suspects with devastating ease.
The pen of a journalist, the mind of a professor, and the heart of
a preacher are here devoted to the service of the King. Macleod's
most accessible Christology to date!'

Dr W. Duncan Rankin
Reformed Theological Seminary,
Jackson, Mississippi

'Those in the know will understand when I say that, whether intended
or not, this book does for the doctrine of the person of Christ what
Professor Macleod's Shared Life has done for the doctrine of the
Trinity; namely, to provide brief but ready access for Christians of
various ecclesial traditions to the richest insights into the profundities
of historic Christian belief. Serious first-time readers of Macleod
cannot but benefit from his remarkable blend of orthodoxy and
creativity, clothed, as it is, in a prose as accessible and illuminating
as it is winsome and compelling. I do not speak with platitudes. Read
for yourself, but, above all, read to glorify the Christ of God!'

Tim J. R. Trumper,
Westminster Theological Seminary

'By his writings and preaching Donald Macleod has already gained
a place among contemporary Christologians. This little book will be
a further valuable resource for all thoughtful and zealous followers
of Christ.

It has the familiar emphases of Macleod's teaching, as he follows the suffering and sin-becoming Saviour, profoundly human and yet inescapably divine, into the shades and darkness of Gethsemane and Calvary. But there are also studies of the Temptation, the Transfiguration, and Jesus' present, heavenly activity and rich and reverent insights into the passionate internal life of the Trinity — the abiding context of the earthly ministry of the Son.

Macleod writes from within the distinctive context of the Free Church of Scotland, and frequently applies Christological truth to the strengths and weaknesses of that particular tradition. But even those who are unfamiliar with the mysteries of General Assemblies, Disruptions, Secessions and Robertson Smiths may be stirred and helped to sift and enrich their own traditions by the truth as it is in Jesus.

Here is the very heart of Christianity. Here is a 'generous orthodoxy', lucidly expounded, honestly defended, and passionately enforced. Here is a book that should equip Christians for ministry, and sharpen our appetites to know more about Jesus.'

John Nicholls,
London City Mission

'Donald Macleod has a unique ability to express complex theological concepts in arresting and thought-provoking language. Not a word is wasted on these pages: as the author explores various aspects of the Person and Work of Jesus Christ, readers will have their minds stretched and their hearts warmed. This book will stimulate discussion, and perhaps even in places provoke heated debate. But it cannot fail to cause us to wonder at the love that provided such a Saviour as we have in Christ.'

Iain D. Campbell,
Back Free Church of Scotland
Isle of Lewis

FROM
GLORY TO GOLGOTHA

CONTROVERSIAL ISSUES IN THE LIFE OF CHRIST

DONALD MACLEOD

CHRISTIAN FOCUS

ISBN 1-85792-718-4

Copyright © Donald Macleod 2002

Published in 2002
by
Christian Focus Publications
Geanies House, Fearn
Ross-shire, IV20 1TW, Great Britain

www.christianfocus.com

Cover Design by Alister MacInnes

Printed in Great Britain by
Cox and Wyman, Reading, Berkshire

CONTENTS

Foreword 7

1. The Word made flesh 9

2. Did Christ have a fallen human nature? 25

3. Was Christ really tempted? 41

4. Did Christ preach himself? 55

5. Towards the cross 69

6. The crucified God 85

7. Why did God sacrifice his own son? 109

8. Jesus and the resurrection 127

9. Did Paul call Jesus God? 139

10. To live is Christ 151

Endnotes 163

FOREWORD

I have little recollection of the circumstances in which any of these pieces were written. I know only that they appeared 'at sundry times and in diverse manners'. Even so, they have a common theme, reflecting a life-time's obsession with Christology. Like all essays they amount only to attempts at understanding, but I hope that while I still have much to learn, I don't have too much to un-learn. At the same time I am more than a little terrified by the thought that the full glory of Christ remains a mystery even to Himself.

1. THE WORD MADE FLESH

Every year the world – and the church – experiences Christmas, that curious amalgam of paganism, commercialism and Christianity which Western civilisation has invented to tide it over the darkest days of the winter. It would be easy to be critical. Yet, in a day of small things, the festive season, so called, has one advantage: it reminds the public of at least the name and the fact of Jesus Christ. The pity is that men seldom go beyond that and that the church itself appears content to leave the supreme mystery of its faith only vaguely hinted at in the glitter and gaiety of what it calls its greatest festival. Christmas is a lost opportunity, a time when the world invites the Church to speak and she blushes, smiles and mutters a few banalities with which the world is already perfectly familiar from its own stock of clichés and nursery rhymes.

The question is still worth asking: What is this Christmas event which everyone hints at but no one talks about? The answer, of course, is the nativity; and the significance of that is defined for us by the Apostle John in one of the greatest statements in the New Testament: 'The Word was made flesh, and dwelt among us, and we beheld his glory, the glory as of the only begotten of the Father, full of grace and truth' (John 1:14).

The Eternal Word

The person of whom John speaks – the Word – is described in the preceding verses of the first chapter of his gospel and the description contains several remarkable features.

First, the Word is eternal. His existence did not begin at Bethlehem. It did not even begin at creation. On the contrary, in the beginning, when everything created came into being, the Word was already in being, unoriginated, uncaused and independent of any other form of existence. There never was when the Word was not. Consequently, the nativity marks not the beginning of Christ's existence but the perforation of history by One from eternity. He is not the product of evolution or the precipitate of a particular genetic inheritance but the intrusion and eruption of the Eternal into the existence of man.

Secondly, the Word was Creator. All things were made by him. He conceived and formulated the creation. He spoke it into being, moulding and building it with a sovereign artistry. This has important consequences both for our view of Christ and for our view of the world. The One who made all things is by definition possessed of awe-inspiring energy and power. He is, in John's view, the Almighty, 'the all-holding' One. Conversely, the ultimate energy is Christ. The creative force, the source of every other form of energy, is not impersonal, blind, capricious or malevolent, but Christlike. The creation expresses him and in itself contains no un-Christlikeness at all. In that confidence we harness its resources, assured that all of them are at least beneficent, and move over every horizon, expecting to find not black holes of sterility and absurdity but coherent and fecund expressions of the mind of Christ.

Thirdly, the Word was God. This is the core of the Christian faith. Without it there could be no incarnation. But what are we really saying when we call Jesus God? We are ascribing to him the greatest divine title of the Old Testament. He is *Elohim*, the God whose name (in the plural form) expresses the most intense and exclusive deity. He is the summation of godhead, the One whose being makes that of all other gods not only superfluous but impossible. But we are also saying that Jesus possesses all the attributes of God. He is eternal, omniscient, unchanging, omnipresent, omnipotent and holy in his mercy, righteousness and love. Beyond that, he performs all the characteristic functions of deity: creation, preservation, government and final judgment. But above all, he enjoys every divine prerogative. The glory due to him is precisely the glory due to God. Every knee is to bow. Every heart is to worship. Every tongue must bless him.

This is the essence of our Christian devotion. The Church is not primarily an evangelistic, preaching community, far less a liturgical, sacramental one. First and foremost it is a community of doxology, of Hallelujahs! and Hosannas!, of bowed heads and adoring song. And that adoration is always Christwards.

Who is he in yonder stall
At whose feet the shepherds fall?
'Tis the Lord! Oh wondrous story!

'Tis the Lord, the King of glory!
At His feet we humbly fall.
Crown Him! Crown Him! Lord of all!

The historic Christian creeds enshrine this doctrine in the statement that Christ is *of one substance* with God the Father. The phrase (*homoousios*) originated with the Greek-speaking Fathers of the ancient Church and was distinguished not only from *heteroousios* (of a different substance) but also from *homoiousios* (of a similar substance). They repudiated energetically not only the idea that Christ was *different* from God but also the idea that he was *like* God. Instead, they insisted that he was God. He lacked nothing that entered into the definition of God. What God was, the Word was.

We must go further still. When we speak of Christ being of the same substance as God, we are not simply affirming a generic identity between Him and the Father, as if they merely belonged to the same species. They are one and the same being: 'I and my Father are one' (John 10:30). Jesus is not a second God additional to the original One. He is Jehovah, the only God, the One who is there.

If this is so, then we must eliminate from our idea of the Saviour's deity every last vestige of subordinationism. Christ, in Calvin's phrase, is *autotheos*. He is God in his own right. He does not derive his being from the Father. Nor is the Father the fountain or principle of his godhead. He possesses the very deity of the Father, including the attribute of self-existence. Otherwise, he could not be the Lord, Jehovah, the Being One.

There remains, however, another factor. The Word was not only God. He was God *with* God. Christ is unreservedly God. But he is not the totality of God. The Father also is God and the Spirit is God. These cannot simply be different names for the same person or different faces of the same person. Otherwise, we could not have the Word with God or the Son sent by God or the Son forsaken by God. Equally, however, they are not different beings, giving us three distinct gods. They are, instead, three eternal distinctions within the One God; but distinctions of such an intensely personal kind that each loves the other and that together they constitute a triune life of which the very essence is love.

Enfleshment

John expresses the idea of incarnation itself
in the phrase 'became flesh'. Two preliminary
points deserve a brief mention.

First, John does not in the least suggest that
in becoming flesh the Word ceased to be what
he was. He was God. He continued to be God,
retaining both his divine identity and his
divine nature. The alternative is unthinkable.
For the Word to have ceased to be divine
would have meant a radical modification in
the very being of God: a reduction from
triuneness to 'bi-uneness'.

Secondly, John speaks of Christ as
becoming flesh. The traditional Christian
expression has been that he *took* or *assumed*
human nature. This is perfectly legitimate –
indeed, it has express biblical warrant: the
Lord *took* the form of a servant (Phil. 2:7).
John's word is bolder and emphasises both
the totalness of the incarnation and the
intimacy between Christ and the flesh. To
have become flesh is to be flesh – a salutary
reminder that humanness is not simply
attached to Christ like a mask or a garment
or an artificial limb. It is something which he
is and through which he effectively expresses
himself.

To proceed then: at the most basic level, the incarnation means that Christ took a true human body, the same in all essential respects as our own. It grew from zygote to foetus to infant to child to adolescent to man. It had the same nutritional and environmental needs. It had the same chemistry, the same anatomy, and the same physiology. It was not an illusion, but was real and tangible. The incarnation was not a theophany – the temporary assumption by God of a human appearance. It was a genuine entering upon the possibility of all those experiences to which our bodies expose ourselves – hunger and thirst, weariness and pain, seeing and hearing, flogging, crucifixion, death and burial.

But the incarnation also meant that the Lord became 'a reasonable soul'. He entered into all the psychological possibilities of human existence. We can view this from at least four different perspectives.

First, he had ordinary human affections, as is shown, for example, by the fact that he had his own friends, choosing twelve of them simply *to be with Him* (Mark 3:14), being especially close to three of them and probably uniquely close to one ('the disciple whom

Jesus loved'). He shows tender consideration for his mother, special affection for the rich young man (Mark 10:21) and compassion for his fellow country-men ('He beheld the city and wept over it').

Secondly, Christ experienced all the ordinary human emotions. He knew sorrow, amazement and grief. He was awestruck by the unfolding providence of God for himself, angered by profanity and fearful of the approach of death.

Thirdly, he had a human faculty of choice. He is incarnate by his own decision. But he must also make decisions as the incarnate One. He chooses to humble himself further, below the level of mere enfleshment (Phil. 2:8). He chooses not to turn stones into bread, not to worship Satan and not to throw himself from the pinnacle of the temple. In Gethsemane, despite profound misgiving and fear, he chooses the cup of sorrow. These are not the effortless, unconditioned decisions of deity, but the painful decisions of humanness made on the basis of limited information by One conscious of creaturely frailty and fearful of the cost.

Fourth, our Lord had a human intellect. Not *only* a human intellect, but *also* a human

intellect. On this human level, there were
things he did not know, the most notable
being the time of his own return in glory:
'Of that day and that hour knows no man,
no, not the angels in heaven, neither the Son,
but the Father' (Matt. 24:36). We should
accept this without embarrassment. The
human nature of Christ was (and is) no more
omniscient than it was omnipotent or
omnipresent. It was at every point dependent:
'Behold my servant, whom I uphold' (Isa.
42:1). This was as true at the intellectual level
as at any other. Christ as man knew only as
much of God (or of his own godhead) as God
was pleased to reveal to him: through general
revelation given in the work of creation and
providence, through special revelation given
in the Scriptures of the Old Testament and
through direct prophetic disclosure given to
him in his capacity as Mediator. Neither
creation nor the Old Testament had anything
to say as to the date of the Second Coming
and Christ could only have known it if God
had given him a special word to that effect.
Instead, the Father chose to keep it 'in his
own power', presumably because this
knowledge had no bearing whatever on the
work of redemption.

We should beware, however, of thinking that this was the only point at which Christ's human knowledge was incomplete. Immeasurably superior as his intellect is to ours, it is not adequate to searching out God. More readily even than Paul's, it cries out before the Glory, 'Oh the depth!', the massive range and superb clarity of its vision serving only to render him more conscious of the immensity of God. The paradox is, of course, that the deity which astonishes him is his own. What he became stands in awe before what he was.

Implication of the incarnation

It follows inescapably from John's doctrine of the incarnation that the Mediator had two natures.

The only way to escape this is to deny either his deity or his humanity or to assert that he was a mongrel fusion of the human and the divine. Two great facts lie at the foundation of our religion: we worship him, and we feel that he is one with us. These demand a two-nature Christology as their basis. Christ has the form of God and the form of a servant; a human mind and a divine mind; human affections and divine affections;

human emotions and divine emotions; a human will and a divine will; human limitedness and divine un-limitedness.

Again, the incarnation is permanent. Christ is still man; or, in John's glorious vision, the Shepherd in the midst of the throne is a Lamb (Rev. 7:17). His humanness has undergone a glorious metamorphosis – it has been *highly exalted* – but it remains humanness, a transfigured amalgam of the dust of the earth and the breath of God (Gen. 2:7). As such, Christ is the sign and the pledge of our own ultimate exaltation: we shall be like him, for we shall see him as he is (1 John 3:2). That is the acme of creaturely development. There can be no evolution of man into something greater than himself. Man is the ultimate, the creature who bears God's image and whose nature God took. Beyond man as he is there is only man as he is to be – man transfigured, conformed to the image of the Son of God.

And dwelt among us
To the doctrine of the enfleshment John adds two further facts.

First, the incarnate Word dwelt among us, identifying completely with our

dependentness and sharing our suffering. His
environment, like ours, was cursed. For him,
too, the ground brought forth thorns and
thistles so that he could eat bread only by the
sweat of his brow. He knew the pain of
bereavement, the pangs of hunger and thirst,
utter physical exhaustion, the malice of
enemies, the faithfulness of friends, public
rejection and humiliation, and the fear of
death. He knew even the pain of an unheeding
heaven and a forsaking God.

Again, he shared with us the experience of
temptation. The devil came at him when he
was hungry and alone. He questioned his
sonship. He plied him with plausible
inducements. He highlighted – even
exaggerated – the cost of obedience. He
obscured the glory of the recompense. He
came through enemies. He came through
friends and apostles. He was given 'his hour',
an hour of special authority when he
unleashes all his violence and uses all his
cunning. In the event, it was all to no avail.
Yet Christ does not reject temptation
effortlessly. He is in an agony and cries
earnestly, the strain such that his perspiration
falls in great bloody drops to the ground. His
sinlessness – his unfallenness – far from

meaning painless temptation means that he never yields and that a repulsed devil must continue his efforts with redoubled force.

Christ also shared our experience of dying: the fact of it, the fear of it, even the taste of it (Heb. 2:9). *Among us* means, at last, between two thieves, crucified, enduring the anathema, his sonship obscured even from himself. At this point, although he is with us (and even for us) we are not with him: 'they all forsook him and fled'. Even the Father is not with him: 'My God, my God, why hast thou forsaken me?' He is among us and without God 'to bring us to God'.

And we beheld his glory

The last thing John says in this verse is, 'We beheld his glory.' In Christ, the glory of God becomes visible. In himself, God is invisible, obscured by impenetrable clouds of otherness; or, alternatively, obscured by brightness which blinds by excess of light. By way of illustration, let us remember that it is impossible to look at the sun with the naked eye. If we make the attempt, we burn the retina and blind ourselves. But it is possible to project an image of the sun backwards through a telescope on to a shaded paper and

then, in that image, to see the features of the
sun itself. So it is with Christ. He is the divine
image, God's word about God. He is the
meaning of the divine attributes, the divine
sovereignty and the divine works. Nowhere
in God – not in his wrath, not in his holiness,
not even in his 'terrible decree' – is there any
contradiction of the image given in the
incarnate One. He is light and in him there is
no darkness – no unChristlikeness – at all.

But that is not all. The glory of God as
defined in Christ has specific characteristics.
It is full of grace and truth. His grace is his
true self – a commitment and concern and
self-effacingness which express the very core
of his being and to which he is unalterably
faithful. Were it otherwise, no man could see
the face of God and live. Now, it is our life to
see him as he is – the glory of God in the face
of Jesus Christ.

2. DID CHRIST HAVE A FALLEN HUMAN NATURE?

The doctrine that Jesus Christ had a true human nature is probably the single most important article of the Christian faith. Indeed, the Apostle John insists that the denial of it is the mark of Antichrist (1 John 4:3). Yet denials there have been, in abundance. In John's own day, the Docetists denied that Christ had a true body. Later, the Apollinarians denied that he had a human spirit and later still Eutychus claimed that he was neither God nor man, but a mixture of both. Less drastically, some later Christian traditions, while not denying the Lord's humanity, spoke in a way which compromised it. Mediaeval Catholicism saw Christ almost exclusively as a remote divine emperor. Lutheranism, because of its insistence on the corporal presence of Christ in the Sacrament, had to formulate the doctrine that His body was ubiquitous, which is hardly consistent with its being a body at all.

It would be arrogant to claim that Reformed theology got it exactly right. But men like Calvin, Owen and Hugh Martin did strive to do justice to the biblical vision of 'the man Christ Jesus' and even the so-called Protestant Scholastics betray no reservations as to the manhood of our Lord. Calvinist theologians – and preachers – have testified, firmly and unambiguously, that Christ took a flesh-and-blood body, possessing the same anatomy and physiology as our own, and linked, through his mother, to the genetic stream of the race. They accepted fully that our Lord experienced such ordinary human emotions as joy, sorrow, fear, amazement and almost-despair. They highlighted his need for companionship, his discriminating friendships (closer to some than to others) and his pained sensitiveness to all the misery around him. They acquiesced unquestioningly in the clear teaching of Scripture that he was temptable and, on some matters, ignorant.

It is arguable, then, that more than any other tradition Reformed theology has sought to be faithful to the claim that Christ is of one and the same substance with us according to his manhood, just as he is of one and the same substance with the Father according to his godhead. Yet the insistence that 'He was in every sense a member of the human race' has its own dangers. As C. F. D. Moule has pointed out, 'According to New Testament writers, the humanity of Jesus is both continuous with and discontinuous from that of the rest of mankind.'[1] The discontinuity is particularly evident at two points. Christ's humanness, unlike ours, was originated supernaturally, in a virgin conception; and Christ's humanness, unlike ours, was sinless.

For the moment, we shall concentrate on the second point. Christ's sinlessness clearly means two things.

First, he was not guilty of any *actual* sin. Never for a moment does he betray any consciousness of having transgressed in word, in emotion, in desire, in ambition or in action. He never, for all his sense of the holy, prays for forgiveness. Nor can we adduce any utterance or incident from his life at which we can point and say, 'There, surely, is a sin!' From within the gospel records he still stands, challenging us, 'Which of you can convict me of sin' (John 8:46). Stated negatively, there is no transgression, no lawlessness, no want of conformity, anywhere in the life of the Saviour. Positively, his whole life is an acted righteousness as he goes out to meet the will of God in an almost aggressive obedience.

Secondly, there was in Christ no *inherent* sin. This again is something on which Scripture is adamant. He was a lamb without blemish and without spot (1 Pet. 1:19), holy, harmless, undefiled and separate from sinners (Heb. 7:26). In stating this we have to avoid compromising his participation in our nature, and the need for careful formulation is clearly seen in such a passage as Romans 8:3, 'God sent forth his Son *in the likeness of sinful flesh.*' We cannot say, 'the likeness of flesh', because that would make his humanness ghost-like – a mere seeming. We cannot say 'sinful flesh' because that would compromise his integrity. We can say that Christ was 'made sin' (2 Cor. 5:21) but we cannot say that he was made sinful. There is no moral or structural defect for Satan to exploit. There is no lust. There is no egotism. There is no proclivity to sin. There is no corruption of nature. There is no want of original righteousness. There is no fallenness.

The same fallen nature as ours?

But this last statement must give us pause. It has become a virtual truism of recent scholarship that 'Christ's human nature was indeed the same fallen human nature as ours'. For the most part, those who hold this view are careful to deny that he was sinful. But they regard it as not only true, but vital, that his humanness was fallen. Otherwise, he could feel no sympathy with us. More fundamentally still, if he did not take fallen human nature, then he did not redeem it.

The credit, if such it is, for the current respectability of this doctrine must go to two men, Edward Irving and Karl Barth.

Irving, an enigmatic and ultimately a tragic figure, was deposed from the ministry of the Church of Scotland in 1833. He never abandoned his own belief in the sinlessness of Christ, but the way he stated it was, to say the least, awkward: Christ's human nature had the *grace* of sinlessness and incorruption. He did not have his sinlessness from himself. He had it only from the indwelling of the Spirit: 'It was manhood fallen which he took up into his divine person, in order to prove the grace and the might of Godhead in redeeming it.'[2] The Lord's humanity was indeed without guilt, but only because it was 'held like a fortress in immaculate purity by the Godhead within'[3].

Barth, too, held to the doctrine of the sinlessness of the Lord: 'Christ was not a sinful man. He did nothing that Adam did.'[4] But he serves himself heir to all that Irving had said of the fallenness of the Saviour's humanity. 'There must,' he says, 'be no weakening or obscuring of the saving truth that the nature which God assumed in Christ is identical with our nature as we see it in the light of the Fall. If it were otherwise, how could Christ be really like us? What concern would we have with Him? We stand before God characterised by the Fall. God's Son not only assumed our nature but he entered the concrete form of our nature, under which we stand before God as men damned and lost.'[5]

Fallen and sinful

It is very doubtful, however, whether the idea that Christ took a fallen human nature can be held meaningfully in any form which is not heretical. There is no practicable distinction between *fallen* and *sinful*. 'Beyond a doubt,' wrote A. B. Bruce, 'the theory requires that original sin should be ascribed to Christ; for original sin is a vice of fallen human *nature*, and the doctrine that our Lord's human nature was fallen, means if it means anything, that it was tainted with original sin.'[6]

The truth of Bruce's claim will appear at once if we recall the teaching of the *Shorter Catechism*: the Fall brought mankind into an estate of sin and misery (Answer 17). To be fallen means not only to be in a state of misery, but to be in a state of sin. And in what does that sinfulness consist? 'The guilt of Adam's first sin, the want of original righteousness and the corruption of (our) whole nature' (Answer 18).

This is really the crux of the matter. A fallen nature means a corrupt nature – indeed, one which is wholly corrupt. Is that what Christ had – a nature which lacked original righteousness and was totally depraved?

Both Irving and Barth strenuously protest their belief in the sinlessness of Christ and we must respect that. But there can be no doubt that as they work out what they mean by a fallen nature they use language which is totally inconsistent with his inherent perfection. As Irving saw it, the flesh which Christ took was one in which 'all sins, infirmities and diseases nestled'. Throughout his life, he had to battle heroically against temptations which sprang, not from the devil, but from his own nature – that 'fragment of the perilous stuff' which he had assumed. The Lord, Irving insists, committed no sinful act. But the possibility of sinning was there and he would have sinned but for the Holy Spirit keeping his flesh under control. He was holy only 'in spite of the law of the flesh working in him as in other men'. What can this mean but that something in him resisted the Spirit – something so powerful that it required the might of the Godhead to keep it in check?

Exactly the same kind of language appears in Barth: *fallen* equals *corrupt*. The flesh which Christ took was 'the concrete form of human nature marked by Adam's fall'. That was not a nature which was good in itself. It was a *vitiated* nature. 'Why does Scripture always speak contemptuously of the flesh unless *corrupt nature* is meant?' Barth quotes a seventeenth century source to the effect that 'it was not fitting that a human nature liable (*obnoxia*) to sin should be united to the Son of God', and comments: 'Not fitting? If that is true, then precisely in the critical definition of our nature, Christ is not a man like us, and so he has not really come to us and represented us.' When we move from Barth's treatment of the Incarnation to his treatment of the Fall of Man, the language only confirms our suspicions. Here, 'the essence of the Fall' is synonymous with 'the situation of man in the state of corruption' and Christ becoming flesh means precisely that he participated in our *corrupted* being.

Discontinuity

In Irving and Barth the link between *fallen* and *corrupt* is not due to any lack of care. The corruptness of the human nature assumed by Christ is precisely what they want to express and the word *fallen* is the ideal word for the purpose. This fact alone is surely sufficient to make its use in evangelical theology thoroughly improper.

There are, however, several other considerations which have a bearing on the question.

First, the plea for total continuity between Christ's humanity and ours is misplaced. The Virgin Birth (which Barth himself defends and expounds so eloquently) is an immediate and unmistakeable reminder of discontinuity. So is the Resurrection: 'The Virgin Birth at the opening and the empty tomb at the close of Jesus' life bear witness that this life is a fact marked off from all the rest of human life.'[7] Christ is the new beginning, the One from outside – outside Adam, outside the Fall, outside guilt, outside corruption. He is God's man, who does not share in the sin of the first man nor in his loss of righteousness nor in the corruption of his nature. So long, indeed, as Christ is without actual sin, Barth cannot have unqualified continuity between him and us. All the rhetoric with which he turns on the unfallenness could be turned equally effectively against the sinlessness. How can he understand if he never sinned? What does he know of shame and sorrow and frustration and failure? What could have been the use to Paul of a Saviour who knew nothing of the anguish behind the words. 'To will is present with me; but how to perform that which is good I find not' (Rom. 7:18)?

The answer is, of course, much use! because the basis of his being 'touched with the feeling of our infirmities' is not that he was either fallen or sinful, but that he shared our nature, our deprivations and our temptations.

Fallenness a disadvantage

Then there is a second – and vital – consideration: To be fallen would be a distinct disadvantage in a Saviour. This is something which becomes totally clear from Barth's own treatment of the Fall of Man. It is Barth himself who quotes Ephesians 2:3, 'We were children of wrath' and goes on to define our fallen nature as one *inclined to hate God and our neighbour*. If that is the nature which Christ took then he, too, was a child of wrath and in no position to save others. When one recalls how emphatically Barth stresses the incapacity of fallen man it is difficult to see how Christ could overcome the disadvantage of having a fallen nature: 'With the Formula of Concord we can call fallen man a stock and a stone in order to describe his whole incapacity to help and save himself.' Did Christ then take upon himself this *whole incapacity*? Again, Barth tells us that the corruption from which God's word of forgiveness calls us 'consists in the fact that man is God's debtor. He is a debtor who cannot pay.'

The cumulative effect of this is overwhelming. Christ took a nature which made him a child of wrath, rendered him incapable of helping himself and turned him into a debtor who could not pay. How can his power to save be salvaged from such wreckage?

A fallen person

Thirdly, it is impossible to speak of Christ having a fallen human nature and yet refrain from describing him as a fallen person. 'If a fallen nature exists at all,' wrote the elder Marcus Dods, 'it can exist only as the nature of a fallen person.'[8] A *nature* is an abstraction. It neither acts nor suffers nor falls. Only persons can fall or be fallen. This is certainly the way theology has traditionally spoken. The Shorter Catechism, for example, does not say that our nature fell. It says that our first parents fell (Answer 13). The Westminster Confession is equally careful: 'By this sin *they* fell from their original righteousness' (ch. VI:II). It was they, not their nature, which became dead in sin and 'wholly defiled in all the faculties and parts of soul and body'.

To say that Adam had a fallen nature is to say that Adam was fallen. The same logic must apply to Christ. If he had a nature that was fallen, then he himself was fallen. The principle of the *communion of attributes* is sufficient to establish this: whatever is true of either nature is true of the person. If the human nature was fallen, the person was fallen.

The implications of this are totally unacceptable to reverent thought. When did Christ fall? In Adam? Or in his own experience? It seems unnecessary to press these points. Christ was one person, one self, one agent, bearing the name, *the Son of God*. To say that the Son of God was fallen is impossible, especially when by fallen we mean 'wholly defiled in all the faculties and parts of soul and body'.

Fallenness not part of humanness

Two other considerations deserve a brief mention.

First, fallenness is no part of the definition of humanness. The underlying motive of Barth's exposition is to maximise the identity between Christ and ourselves. As he sees it, the denial of fallenness jeopardises this: 'precisely at the critical definition of our nature Christ is not a man like us.' The answer to that, surely, is that to be fallen is not part of what defines our nature. If it were, then the newly created Adam was not a man.

Indeed, on these terms God did not create a man at all. What he created only became a man by falling. The same conclusion would apply at the other end of human destiny. Glorified man would not be human – certainly not in 'the concrete form of our nature marked by Adam's fall'.

Finally, those who argue that Christ had a fallen human nature misconceive the reason for his sufferings. The Lord suffered in every dimension of his existence; physically, socially, emotionally and spiritually. Furthermore, the agony which this involved brought him to the very limits of his human endurance. Even though upheld by the Spirit he is at last close to being overwhelmed.

But the reason for his suffering was not that he was fallen. It was, instead, that he was the Vicar of the fallen. He was their Representative and Substitute. He was under *their* curse, sharing *their* low estate. His liability to the anathema is not personal. It is contractual. As to himself, he has no debts. He is meeting the debts of others. His manhood has become the place of judgment – the very Gehenna to which all the world's guilt is gathered. He is the Holocaust consumed by God's anger against sin. But the sin is not his own. It is never, in any sense, inherent. He is the atonement for the fallenness of others.

It is superficial to imagine that this unfallenness protected him from the highest levels of pain. On the contrary, it made him uniquely vulnerable. A Nazi could have walked unmoved through Belsen. Bonhöeffer could not. He would have been moved to the depths of his being by the misery and the criminality. In the same way Christ moved among men with an exquisite, unfallen sensitiveness to the pain, the squalor, the oppression and the degradation around him. He had to live amid the manifestations of sin, see it, hear it, feel it, everywhere; suffer for it, bear it – at last, take his very name from it (2 Cor. 5:21). And how could he bear the loss of God? To the fallen, that is a familiar and not altogether unwelcome experience. To Christ, living eternally with God and towards God, it was an unspeakable horror. In prospect, it filled him with overwhelming fear. In actuality, it rendered him desolate. The Far Country was infinitely more harrowing for the Only Begotten than for the Prodigal.

That, we said, was the final consideration. But the most important thing of all remains unsaid. Surely if he was unfallen, Christ could not have been tempted. That, unfortunately, cannot be dealt with in a few sentences. But we will discuss it in the next chapter.

3. WAS CHRIST REALLY TEMPTED?

In the previous chapter, we looked briefly at the question whether Christ's human nature was fallen, arguing that it was not. To many minds, however, this immediately suggests a difficulty: How then could he be tempted?

There can be no denying the reality of the Lord's temptations. The New Testament pointers are too explicit. He was led into the desert to be tempted by the devil (Mark 1:12). He can help those who are tempted only because he himself has been tempted (Heb. 2:18). And his temptations, although without sin, were exactly like those of his brethren (Heb. 4:15).

In every instance the temptation was repelled and our Lord remained sinless. But he did not win these victories effortlessly. In the desert, the struggle is preceded by a long fast. At Caesarea Philippi, when Peter becomes the devil's mouthpiece, the Lord's rebuke ('Get thee behind me, Satan!') is so sharp as to suggest that the temptation has struck a raw nerve. In Gethsemane, the agony of resistance is so intense that the Lord sweats great drops of blood and cries to God with strong crying and tears. At last, indeed, God's will is embraced, and done. But the temptation is not repelled easily and automatically. On the contrary, the narrative conveys the very distinct impression that the Lord has to summon all his resources, internal and external, to repel this last great attack of the adversary.

Foothold?

But what foothold would temptation have found in Christ? What was the point of contact?

We cannot accept the premise that only fallen or sinful beings can be tempted. Unless we are to believe that God actually *created* sinners, we must hold that sin is the result of temptation rather than temptation the result of sin. This was certainly the case with the First Adam. As originally created, he was 'good' and 'upright'. Only through temptation did he fall into sin, and that temptation was itself entirely external. Adam was not morally and spiritually neutral. He was positively holy; and yet temptable. It was the same with Christ. The prince of this world had nothing in him (John 14:30). There was no evil passion to mortify and no sinful proclivity to which temptation could address itself.

Where, then, did Satan find a point of contact? The answer must be, surely, in his humanness. His humanness had no vices, but it did have deep basic instincts, he was perfectly sinless. He could not, simultaneously, gratify those instincts *and* obey. He had to choose: and it was the necessity of such choice which made temptation possible.

It would be irreverent to probe too deeply into what these instincts were. But there are some things which can be safely deduced from the gospel narrative.

For example, the Lord had an ordinary human need for food and it was this which made possible his first temptation in the desert. Equally he had human social instincts and these would lead him to shrink from any course of action which would distress his family and friends. For the same reason, he would dread a line of duty which involved, at last, utter friendlessness and loneliness. Again, he instinctively shrank from sin. Yet his duty meant intimate involvement with it. He must live among sinners. He must be identified with them, and be reputed one of them. At last he would be dealt with simply as a sinner. It was not unholiness to shrink from that.

On a deeper level still, there was a point of contact for the Tempter in the Saviour's love for God. From eternity he had been with God, seeing his face and being assured of his love. To fear the loss of these things – to be tempted to avoid losing them – was no sin. The temptation would be strong precisely in proportion to his holiness. He trembled before the cross not only from ordinary instincts of self-preservation but from the terrible knowledge that it meant not simply death but the loss of God – God, whom he had never lost before, and in whose company he had gone up, 'both of them together', from Bethlehem to Calvary. We may almost say: it would have been a sin not to be tempted to put away the cup. Such a desire was no vice, but 'a holy passion to restrain'.

Reducing the pain?

But would the fact of being sinless not significantly reduce the pain of temptation for our Lord, put him at a distance from us and place him exactly where Hebrews 4:15 insists he should not be placed – where He could not be 'touched with the feeling of our infirmities'?

Three comments must suffice.

First, some measure of distance between Christ and us is inevitable so long as we cling to the doctrine that he was sinless. This appears clearly if we consider the words of James 1:14, 'Every man is tempted when he is lured and enticed by his own lust: then when lust has conceived, it brings forth sin.' This is the invariable rule of temptation so far as men are concerned. But it does not apply to Christ. Our temptations begin within ourselves. This is not a matter merely of the Tempter having a point of contact in our own depravity. It is much more radical than that. Our lusts initiate the sinful action. They suggest, motivate and propel. Christ knew nothing of that. He was tempted not as one fallen but as one on probation – one who survived and never fell. In his case, the true parallel and contrast is not with us, but with the First Adam. Like him, he was tempted. Unlike him, he stood. That means inevitably that Christ does not understand fallenness from the inside. But that is not a fact to be regretted. His fall would have been his failure as a Saviour.

Secondly, it is doubtful whether Christ himself always knew that his victory was assured. Objectively, of course, the fact was beyond dispute. He was the Son of God, he was working out the purposes of God and he was upheld by God. He could not conceivably have failed. In his darkest moments, however, that assurance was probably not present to his human consciousness. In the desert, the Tempter puts a question mark against the sonship itself. The Cross eclipses it: for once, He is unable to say, 'Abba, Father!' and cries, instead, 'My God, my God!' The certainty of victory was liable to be eclipsed in the same way as the Lord wrestled with particular temptations. There is an analogy here with the life of the believer. We enjoy assurance of salvation and certainty of perseverance, but this does not eliminate fear and anxiety as we face the devil's attacks.

Thirdly, it is completely misguided to imagine that the agony of temptation overcome is less than the agony of temptation yielded to. On the contrary, to yield to temptation is to escape its full ferocity. The devil never has to do his utmost to secure *our* fall. A little of his power and cunning will suffice. But Christ did not yield and this made it necessary for the Tempter to increase the pressure. Here, for the one and only time, he had to try everything he knew, using every means, every agent and every occasion. He stepped up the intensity to an appalling pitch: but still Christ did not yield. From this point of view there is an interesting contrast between the temptations in the desert and the agony in Gethsemane. In the desert, there is an imperious rejection of the Tempter's suggestions. In Gethsemane, there is agony. Certainly, there is victory, but in a way that leads us to interject always, *ultimately*. *Ultimately*, there is victory. He was almost overwhelmed, almost broken, so that he had to cry with strong crying and tears. Far from being the One who escapes temptation because he is sinless, he is the one who precisely because he is sinless alone experiences temptation in its full intensity. He alone took all the devil could throw at him.

The devil's aim

What were the precise points at which the devil aimed?

First, the Lord was tempted as to his sonship. At one level, the issue raised here was simply whether he was the Son at all: 'If you are the Son of God!' The devil could certainly point out that the facts of the Lord's life could not support any such assurance. He had no bread. He had no kingdom. His sonship was hidden. All that men could see was a man, 'without form or comeliness', 'a root out of dry ground'. At times, possibly, that was also all that the Lord himself could see, particularly when his glory is obliterated under the darkness of Calvary.

But there may, as Karl Barth suggested, be something deeper: the temptation to be obsessed with the question of his own sonship.[1] The third temptation in the desert revolves around the question of a sign: if the Lord throws himself from the pinnacle of the temple, the angels will bear him up and he will sustain no injury. It is often assumed that what is envisaged here is some demonstrative portent to impress others with the glory of Christ. But as Barth points out, there were no others present. The sign was a sign for himself, for his own reassurance. The temptation was of the utmost gravity: to say, 'The real question is my own sonship – to make sure of that and forget all else and all others and all service until that is absolutely clear'. It is a temptation to which all of us are liable and to which the only answer is the attitude of John Bunyan, prepared to die for the gospel, 'come heaven, come hell'.[2] Obsession with the question of our own salvation is sometimes only a Satanic egotism.

Secondly, the Lord was tempted as to his self-renunciation. The very meaning of the incarnation, especially as defined in Philippians 2:7, was that 'Christ made himself nothing'. He did not cling to his rights, but consented to becoming a man of no consequence, whom no one acclaimed. He put his own interests aside to concentrate entirely on the interests of others. Time and again the tempter attacked him at this point. He is tempted to protect himself and to declare himself and, above all, to step out from among the sinners with whom he had identified in baptism. This is already the devil's aim in the first temptation: He must refuse the experience of hunger, or at least dependence on ordinary sources of supply. Significantly, the Lord's answer begins with the word *man*: '*man* shall not live by bread alone'. That is what he is — a man; and he must accept not only the appearance but the reality, including hunger and dependence.

The same strategy lies behind the other two temptations in the desert and behind Peter's vehement rejection of the idea that the Lord could be crucified (Mark 8:32). But it is in Gethsemane that the final, full-scale assault is mounted. Here the Lord must face the full implications of his renunciation in all their urgency and imminence. The humiliation was not a point, but a line along which the Lord must move from Bethlehem to Baptism, from Baptism to Gethsemane, from Gethsemane to Calvary. Yet it was not as if anything that had gone before was a preparation for Calvary. There was no gradual build-up. Calvary was new: the extremes of physical pain, death and loneliness; above all, the loss of God. Hitherto he had never been alone. The Father had always been with him. But soon: he would be sin, he would be in the Far Country, he would face that wholly unpreparable-for moment when God was not there. In Gethsemane, there was still time to draw back and the arguments for such a course were strong. How could love face the loss of love? *Should* love face the loss of love? Even choose it? He is despondent; close to despair. He is afraid. He is almost overwhelmed. But he stands. He takes the cup. He confirms and re-enacts his decision to be nothing. And he faces the cross – damnation and anathema – with invincible resolution: 'Rise up, let us go.' From that point onwards, there is not a falter.

Is there not something in the change of mood represented by the contrast between John's account of the Upper Room and the other evangelists' account of Gethsemane? In the Upper Room, just before Gethsemane, the Saviour is relaxed and confident, as if the ordeal were already behind him: 'I have finished the work given me to do.' In the garden, he is distraught: 'Let this cup pass from me!' In that sudden change, is there not our own most authentic humanness? What at one moment seems so easy as to be negligible, we face the next moment in sheer terror.

Resources
The older theologians made much of the fact that Christ survived temptation because his human nature was supported by his divine

nature. It is doubtful, however, whether this reflects the biblical way of looking at things. Strictly speaking, natures do not act. It is persons who act. So far as Scripture is concerned, it was not the divine nature, but God the Father acting through the Spirit, who sustained the Mediator: 'Behold my servant, whom I uphold... I have put my Spirit upon him' (Isa. 42:1). To speak of one nature in Christ supporting the other is to come perilously close to Nestorianism (the heresy which so distinguished the two natures as to make Christ virtually two persons).

It also seems worth noting that Christ did not simply suffer temptation. He was specifically led – even driven into it – by the Holy Spirit. He had to take a positive initiative in launching the attack on the Kingdom of Darkness. Karl Barth may even be right in suggesting that that was a day and an encounter the devil would rather have avoided. He could not have relished a contest with the Son of God.

The Sequel
Finally, the sequel to the temptation. For one thing, there was a period of some relief: 'the devil left him for a while' (Luke 4:13).

Furthermore there was a time of increased comfort: angels ministered to him (Mark 1:13), no doubt strengthening him as one of them did later in Gethsemane. Above all, the temptations were followed by increased usefulness. He returned to Galilee in the power of the Spirit and commenced the public ministry which was to continue, without intermission, to the end. There was no time to rest on his laurels.

Nor can there be for us. Temptation does not exempt from duty or justify delay in attending to it. We cannot even ask for time to recover. Gethsemane is followed not by the rest but by Calvary. 'Rise up, let us go.'

4. DID CHRIST PREACH
HIMSELF?

In a way that is unique among the religions of the world, Christ is central to his own teaching. At least, this is the impression given by the historic creeds of Christendom and by the behaviour and protestations of Christians down through the centuries. It is also the impression conveyed by the earliest Christian preaching as recorded in the New Testament. Peter's sermon on the day of Pentecost, for example, has as its theme, 'Jesus of Nazareth, a man approved among you by God in miracles, wonders and signs' (Acts 2:22). The same applies to the sermon preached before Cornelius (Acts 10:34-42): 'God commanded us to preach to the people and to testify that Christ is the one who was ordained by God to be the judge of the living and the dead.'

The point need not be laboured. The whole essence of New Testament Christianity is expressed in the affirmation of Paul, 'For me to live is Christ' (Phil. 1:21). 'Early Christian theology,' wrote Oscar Cullmann, 'is in reality almost exclusively Christology.'[1]

Some scholars argue, however, that there is a radical difference here between developed Christianity and the attitude of Jesus himself. 'The Gospel as Jesus proclaimed it,' according to Adolf Harnack, 'has to do with the Father only and not with the Son.' He continues: 'A great departure from what Christ thought and taught is involved in putting a Christological creed in the forefront of the Gospel.'[2] Rudolf Bultmann, predictably, is of the same opinion: 'He who formerly had been the *bearer* of the message was drawn into it and became its content. *The proclaimer became the proclaimed*'[3] (italics his). For Bultmann, there is a generic difference between the message of Jesus and the theology of the New Testament. 'Christian faith', he writes, 'did not exist until there was a Christian kerygma; i.e., a kerygma proclaiming Jesus Christ to be God's eschatological act of salvation. He was first so proclaimed in the kerygma of the earliest church, not in the message of the historical Jesus.'[4]

Unfortunately, history contains no evidence of the existence of a Christ such as that of Harnack and Bultmann. The only extant records of the life and teaching of Jesus are the Gospels and in all of these – as well as in their sources, so far as we can identify them – he is portrayed as bearing witness to himself, as claiming the unqualified allegiance of men and as fully conscious of his own pre-temporal and divine uniqueness.

The Great Thanksgiving

Take, for example, the great thanksgiving recorded in Matthew 11:25-30. Nobody who thought he was even remotely ordinary could have uttered these words.

First of all, Jesus, as he understands himself, sustains a unique relation to God. This is clear from the unqualified way he uses the designations 'the Father' and 'the Son'. There is only one person who can conceivably be called 'the Father', and, equally, there is only one person – himself – who can conceivably be called 'the Son'. The usage is not peculiar to this passage. It occurs also in the statement, 'Of that day and that hour knows no man, no, not the angels in heaven, nor the Son, but only the Father' (Matt. 24:36; Mark 13:32). These passages are especially significant because their explicit disavowal of omniscience on the part of our Lord places them above critical suspicion. Even the most sceptical would be hard-pressed to deny that we stand here on a sure historical foundation. The Jesus of history, no less than the Christ of dogma, was 'the Son'.

Secondly, Christ lays claim to a unique knowledge of God. Not only does he say that 'no one knows the Father except the Son and anyone to whom the Son chooses to reveal him' but he also says that 'all things have been delivered to him by the Father.' There can be little doubt but that when Christ speaks of the things which the Father delivered to him, he has specifically in mind the revelation of God – the things which have been hidden from the wise and prudent but revealed to Christ and by him in turn to 'the babes'. *All things* meant a complete revelation. Not that the disclosure was exhaustive. It was not – and could not be – an unveiling to men of the totality of God. Even the revealed God must remain hidden in many aspects of his glory. There are depths in his being which man – even in the humanity of Christ – is not able to search out and would not be able to comprehend even if they were revealed. But God has given us in Christ a revelation of all that we need to know in order to our salvation. He has disclosed what he has prepared for those who love him (1 Cor. 2:9-10), the *mystery* of his decision to exercise clemency and show pity to a lost race. He has declared how he has given effect to that decision, to what consummation he will carry it and what he requires of us in order that we may enjoy it. But that knowledge is in Christ exclusively. No other religious leader has it – their formulations are darkness (Matt. 4:16; Eph. 3:18). Nor does any other person within Christ's own religion have it. His knowledge is of a different order from that of prophet or apostle. Theirs is derivative – and derivative from him. Their commission is to teach all nations whatever he has commanded (Matt. 28:20). He, by contrast, is the source both of the Old Testament revelation (1 Pet. 1:11) and of the apostolic message (1 Cor. 1:23; 15:1, Gal. 1:2ff.).

As he understands himself, then, Christ has both a unique relation to God and an utterly exclusive knowledge of God. Furthermore, he himself is so far an enigma that only the Father knows him: 'no man knows the Son, but the Father.' The same point is brought out in the story of Peter's confession. It is not due to any natural insight or acuteness that Peter is able to assert the true identity of Jesus as the Messiah and the Son of God: 'flesh and blood hath not revealed it unto you, but my Father who is in heaven' (Matt. 16:17). Ordinary perceptions could, of course, grasp some of the reality. It knew his connections ('Is not this the carpenter!') and could even be amazed by the authority with which he taught (Matt. 7:28f.). But as he understands himself there was a mystery behind which flesh and blood could not penetrate; a secret known only to the Father and those to whom the Father revealed it. The reasons for this are not, for the moment, important. What matters is that it shows so clearly that in the judgement of Christ himself those who saw only his outward life and conduct knew very little about him. The mystery of his identity and function was not open to unaided human perception. His most intimate disciples penetrated the mystery only intermittently and partially and even when they came closest to him he remained *Deus absconditus* (the hidden God). All men could know his putative father, mother and brothers. But, as he saw himself, no created mind knew the mystery of his begetting, the greatness of his glory or the delight which the Father had in him.

One further point should be noted from this passage, namely, the consciousness of unique eminence and competence which lies behind the invitation of verse 28. Men, as Christ sees them, are weary and heavy-laden. They are the victims of economic, social and religious oppression. They lack contentment and security. That is Christ's diagnosis and we may readily concede that he was neither the first nor the last to make it. But Christ goes beyond diagnosis. He has a cure and that, surely, is stupendous enough. But he even goes beyond that. He is himself the cure: Come unto *Me*. As he understands himself he can offer rest to the whole world – to every man, woman and child. Fully conscious of the magnitude of the problem and visibly so frail and vulnerable, he offers the world redemption from its tyrannies and deliverance from its neuroses.

The conditions of discipleship

This passage, then, provides firm evidence of what Sydney Cave called 'this colossal consciousness of sonship'.[5] But the impression is confirmed by a host of other details from the Synoptic gospels. For example, no ordinary human being could have insisted on such an attitude to himself as Christ prescribes in Matthew 10:37-39. The passage is so familiar that it is easy to be blind to its implications. Christ expected of his disciples total consecration and unqualified self-denial. He demands that men sacrifice their family-lives for him, leaving father and mother, brother and sister, for his sake. Men must even be prepared to lay down their lives for him and his gospel. Indeed, no one is worthy of him who does not follow him with – in the graphic words of James Denney – 'the rope around his neck, ready to die the most ignominious death rather than prove untrue.'[6] Even more stupendously, he dares to say that men's everlasting destiny depends on their attitude to him. To save one's life at the cost of denying him is to lose it. Conversely, to lose one's life for him is to save it. These words are as well-attested as any in the New Testament, occurring in Mark (8:34ff.), in John (12:25), in Luke (17:33) and in Matthew (10:37). We have no reason to regard them as creations of the early church – indeed, if Jesus did not speak words of this kind the life of the early church is inexplicable. Nor have we any reason to suppose that they exaggerate in any way the claims which Jesus made (and still makes) on his disciples. And whatever may be our final judgment of the person who spoke them they certainly indicate that to his own mind he was related as no other could be to the purposes of God and to the lives of men.

Furthermore, Jesus accepted men's faith and worship even when it was most enthusiastic and, from a human point of view, idolatrous and even blasphemous. One of the most striking instances of this is the story of the healing of the centurion's servant (Luke 7:6-10). Not only did the centurion believe that Jesus could heal but he believed that it was not necessary for him to attend in person. This in turn rested on his conviction that Jesus had at his disposal a host of spiritual messengers in the same way as an officer in the Roman army had at his beck and call a staff of slaves and soldiers. The important point is that Jesus enthusiastically welcomed this attitude: 'I have not found such great faith, no, not in Israel.' He does not protest against the ascription of worship to a creature as Paul does in Acts 14:15 and the angel does in Revelation 22:9. He welcomes faith not only in the Father but in himself as one equal with the Father.

Again, Christ is central in the distinctive sacrament of the New Covenant. The reliability of the tradition is hardly open to question at this point and few would deny that the Supper goes back to the Lord's own institution and intention. It is equally clear that in both the Pauline and Synoptic accounts Christ is the focal point of the ordinance. It is in remembrance of Christ. It is a showing forth of his death. It is a symbol of remission by his blood. It is an act of communion with him. It is partaken of 'till He come'. 'No Christian faith,' if we may quote James Denney again, 'ever put Jesus in a more central and demanding position than this.'[7]

The same conclusion follows from an examination of the Sermon on the Mount and particularly of the so-called great antitheses (Matt. 5:21-48). The authenticity of these antitheses is seldom doubted. More important is the question of the position from which the Lord is dissenting. Many assume that he is setting himself over against the teaching of the Old Testament. But his own language in the immediately preceding context makes such an interpretation of his intention impossible: 'Think not that I am come to destroy the law or the prophets: I came not to destroy but to fulfil.' What Christ is repudiating is the legalism and hypocrisy of the Pharisaic tradition, which by its casuistical evasions and concessions had removed the stringency from 'the royal law' of love. The significant fact for our present purpose, however, is not that Jesus issues these great challenges to rabbinism but that he legislates simply and entirely on his own authority. This was what struck his audience most forcibly. He taught as one who had authority, and not as the scribes. He bases his teaching not on the sayings of predecessors nor on the authority of Moses nor even on a 'thus saith the Lord', but exclusively on his own word. As he repudiates some of the master-principles of Pharisaism, and imposes on his own followers an ethic of awesome rigour, he does not deem it necessary to appeal to any authority beyond, 'I say unto you.' He stands altogether above the tradition and assumes as a right the unconditional and implicit submission of his people. The fact that *he says* is enough to institute and enough to abrogate.

Even more striking is the understanding of his own person and ministry which emerges towards the close of the sermon and especially in Matthew 7:21-23. These words clearly assume that Christ will be the judge of men and the final arbiter of human destiny: 'Many will say to *Me* in that day ...'. Furthermore, as he sees it, it will be perfectly appropriate (although it will not be enough) that men then will address him as 'Lord, Lord.' Beyond that, it is he who will assign his doom to each and pronounce the solemn words, 'Depart from me, ye that work iniquity.' And beyond that still, the criterion which will be applied is men's relation to *him*. A soul will be lost because 'I never knew you'. This last point is made even more forcibly in Matthew 25:31-46, where Christ is represented as the Son of Man sitting on the throne of his glory with all nations gathered before him. Here, too, Christ is the one who assigns to each his destiny, separating the sheep from the goats and pronouncing either, Come! or Depart! and here again the criterion is a man's relation to him: 'I was hungry, and you gave *me* meat.' We may seem, at first sight, to be very far from the dogma of the deity of Christ when we assert simply that he is the appointed judge of all men. But a moment's reflection will remind us that this position requires such a degree of spiritual insight, such discernment of the thoughts and intents of the heart and such awesome moral supremacy as are possible to God alone. 'The imagination,' wrote H. P. Liddon, 'recoils in sheer agony from the task of contemplating the assumption of these duties by any created intelligence.'[8]

John the Baptist

It is interesting to compare the attitude of Jesus with that of John the Baptist. John, most emphatically, did not preach himself. He saw himself as Messiah's forerunner whose duty it was to prepare his way. His whole demeanour, in accordance with this, is one of humility and self-effacement. He directs attention away from himself, protesting that he is not the Christ and that one comes after him whose shoelaces he is not worthy to untie.

The consciousness of Jesus is utterly different. As he sees himself, he has a unique mission, a unique knowledge, a unique authority and, above all, a unique relation to God. He claims total loyalty and commitment and accepts without embarrassment the highest veneration and adoration. In the abstract, Christ may have been wrong in so assessing himself. There can be no doubt, however, but that this is how he did assess himself. The cult of Jesus, which is so prominent in the Pauline Epistles and in the writings of John, is in perfect accord with the self-consciousness of Christ as portrayed in the Synoptic gospels. Indeed, unless Christ had so understood himself it is doubtful whether the epistles (or the Church) could ever have existed.

5. TOWARDS THE CROSS

One of the most remarkable features of the gospel story is the buildup towards the cross. It begins with the announcement of Caesarea Philippi: 'The Son of Man must suffer many things and be rejected by the elders and by the chief priests and scribes and be killed' (Mark 8:31-3). At that point the cross already seems imminent. Yet other events of huge moment lie between, notably the Transfiguration, the Foot-Washing and Gethsemane. These are fascinating in their own right. Yet their meaning does not lie in themselves. They draw almost all their significance from their connection with the cross.

The Transfiguration

As has often been pointed out, the cross is set between the Transfiguration on the one side and the Empty Tomb on the other. That setting is essential to its meaning. It is the cross of the Transfigured One, the Son of God; and it is the cross of the Risen One, whom death could not hold. These facts rule out any interpretation which suggests that all we have here is a poignant human tragedy or a mere act of martyrdom. The setting is fraught with paradox: the death of the Immortal. But it is also filled with hope: the death of the Risen One. Any interpretation which fails to do justice to either of these facts stands condemned.

But the Transfiguration was not in the first instance God's gift to interpreters. It was one of the outstanding moments in the Father's ministry to the Son: an indispensable moment of encouragement.

How was the encouragement administered? Most obviously, through the central event itself: 'He was transfigured before them.' His form was changed. This was saying three things to the Lord.

First, it reminded him of his own essential, underlying glory. During almost his entire ministry on earth that glory was veiled. There was nothing about him to indicate who he really was. He was, to use Luther's phrase, *incognito*. People saw only an ordinary human being: indeed, one less than ordinary, his human frailty exaggerated by poverty, homelessness, pain and rejection. Inevitably this affected the way he saw himself. His assurance of his own sonship was liable to Satanic attack: *If* you are the Son of God (Matt. 4:3). But on the Mount of Transfiguration a momentary reminder is given of the glory that is really his. The ordinariness is replaced by extraordinariness as his whole person is irradiated by the most intense whiteness: the symbol of the God who is Light. For a moment, his appearance and his circumstances befit his status as the Son of God: a reminder, on the threshold of the cross, that although death had a right to him as the Sin-Bearer, it could have no authority to hold him.

Secondly, the Transfiguration is a foretaste of the transformation, beyond the cross, of his own humanness. On earth, his humanness suffers aggravated indignity, far beyond the common range of sorrow, deprivation and pain. On the cross it will suffer such abuse as to be scarcely recognisable even as human: 'His appearance was so disfigured beyond that of any man and his form marred beyond human likeness' (Isa. 52:14). That torn, lacerated, dehydrated body and that broken,

bleeding, battered face constitute an
impenetrable barrier to recognition. None of
the glory can be seen: not even by himself.
But in the Transfiguration, Christ is given a
glimpse of the exaltation and transformation
which lie beyond his agony. He will be an
equal partner in the sovereignty of God (Rev.
5:6). He will share in the glory the Eternal
Word had beside the Father before the world
was made. His poor, abused body will be so
transformed that in it men will see the very
glory of God. In that body, matter – the earth
and its elements – will find its Omega Point
in an organism of unsurpassable beauty,
efficiency and majesty. The resurrection body
will be the supreme achievement of the Great
Maker.

Thirdly, the Transfiguration gave Christ
a glimpse of what his death would mean for
his people. Not only he, but they, would be
transfigured. They would bear his image
(Rom. 8:29). Their bodies would be as
glorious as his (Phil. 3:21). They would fully
share his glory (John 17:24). Like their Lord
they experience this world as a place where
they live *incognito*. Men cannot recognise
them (1 John 3:1) and sometimes they cannot
recognise themselves. Their sonship, like his,

is veiled by their circumstances; and unlike his, by their sins. But one day, beyond the cross and because of the cross, they too will be transfigured and come to bear the image and the likeness and the form and the glory of the Son of God. God will present them to himself faultless (Jude 24); and he will do it with inexpressible joy, seeing in each one of the Redeemed the exact image of his Son.

That, perhaps, was the supreme encouragement for our Lord. He had come into the world under the impulse of love, to serve and to save. The great word spoken on the Mount is that his death will not be a waste or a futility. It will sow the seed of a new Mankind.

But the change in his own form was not the only encouragement held out to our Lord. The Mount of Transfiguration also witnessed an appearance of Moses and Elijah. What was their ministry in relation to the cross? How did they encourage the Lord in the face of his ordeal? All we are told is that they discussed his death. But that itself is enough. The disciples had refused to hear mention of the matter. Don't talk nonsense! they had said (Matt. 16:22). That must have been profoundly discouraging to Jesus. The central purpose of his life, and those closest to him wouldn't even talk about it! But Moses and Elijah would. Two of the greatest figures of the Old Testament. Two men, each of whom had been in his own way a Saviour: Moses at the Exodus and Elijah on Mount Carmel. Two saints already glorified, one without tasting death and the other tasting it only in mysteriously modified form. And they didn't regard Messiah's death as unmentionable. They owed their all to it. They mentioned their gratitude for it. They told him how his mission was regarded with wonder in heaven. How its climax was awaited with bated breath. How the angels peered down (1 Pet. 1:12), spellbound. How the Father was so moved. How the Spirit was so involved. How indescribably extravagant the glory his death secured. It will be an Exodus in comparison to which mine was but a shadow, said Moses. A victory in comparison to which mine was as nothing, said Elijah. And of course they shared with him heaven's certainty as to the outcome.

But there was a voice even more important that the voice of Moses and Elijah: 'A voice came from the cloud, This is my beloved Son, with whom I am well pleased.' The outstanding thing here is that the encouragement comes from God the Father. Sometimes the church has spoken as if the support received by Christ on earth consisted of strength imparted to his human nature from his divine. The divine nature upheld the human, it was said. But this is not the way scripture puts it. The Bible puts it in terms of one Person helping another: 'Behold my servant whom I uphold, my chosen one in whom my soul delights' (Isa. 42:1). This is the pattern we find in the Transfiguration: the Father following his Son with loving solicitude and moving in at the critical moment with words of reinforcement and encouragement.

There is a deliberate emphasis, too, on the glory of the source from which the encouragement came. It came from within the cloud. From Sinai to the Parousia, the Cloud is the great sign of the Presence. Peter brings out its meaning fully: the voice came from the Excellent Glory. Men despise the humiliated Christ. The disciples are ashamed of the cross. But the Excellent Glory honours him as his own Son and proclaims his love. In the gathering darkness the Father reminds

him who he is and how precious he is to
heaven.

The foot-washing

So far as its connection with the cross is
concerned, the story of the foot-washing
(John 13:1-17) is remarkable chiefly for what
it tells us of the Lord's mental state as the
final crisis approached. Three thoughts
occupied his mind.

First, he knew that 'his hour' had come:
the hour of his own agony. He knew that very
shortly he would be betrayed and arrested.
He would be accused of a capital crime. He
would be flogged. He would be crucified. He
would face pain beyond the most awful reach
of his imagination. Reason enough, one would
have thought, for the Lord to be pre-occupied.
Certainly we ourselves are adept at making
our own pain an excuse for not paying much
attention to the needs of others. But the great
thing in the story of the foot-washing is that
as the Lord stands knowingly on the threshold
of his own torment, the one thing that grips
him is this, 'These men are tired! Their feet
haven't been washed.'

What a great lesson it is! Sometimes a
Christian may be called to serve others, even

though blinded by his own tears. Bereft, to comfort them. Weak, to strengthen them. Trembling, to reassure them. Sometimes, distracted by a thousand cares, we must attend to the intricacies of ministry; or, wracked by doubt ourselves, seek to relieve the torment of others. It is so easy to make our own needs – our own 'hour' – an excuse for not serving. Can't you see I have enough! Can't you see I'm busy! Can't you see my pain! my burdens! That is exactly what Christ did *not* say. In his own hour he was available for others.

Secondly, the Lord's mind was pre-occupied with love for his own: 'Having loved his own which were in the world, he loved them unto the end.'

At one level, loving to the end simply meant that his love never faltered and never gave up. Yet they weren't easy people to love. They were so unteachable and so uncomprehending. Their vision was so earthbound. They were so self-centred. And as the crisis deepened, things only got worse. They denied him. They fled. They lost all faith in him. Yet he loved them through all the disappointments. His love was not blind. Imaging forth the love of the Eternal Himself it knew the worst about them: and us. But it survived every discovery and, in full knowledge of our obduracy and fickleness, mounted the cross to save us.

But there is a deeper meaning. He loved us to the end – to the extreme limit – of what love was going to cost. The essential nature of his mission was clear to Jesus from the first. But he would grasp the full meaning of his destiny only gradually, through the months and years of reflection on the scriptures, prayerful communion with the Father and sustained pondering of the gravity of sin. By the time of the foot-washing he is as close as reflection and imagination can bring him to understanding his own sufferings. He knows what his love is going to cost. Yet he is prepared to go to the very limit of that cost. He knows that love will mean unimaginable physical pain. He knows that it will mean experiencing the spiritual torments of the condemned and ruined man. He will become sin. He will be dealt with as sin deserves. He will become the Holy Place where the sin of the whole world will be condemned. It will be condemned in his body, cursed in his Person. There will be no sparing. He will become the one Outside, the Great Outsider. He will be forsaken by God, not heard when he cries, not comforted in his pain. He will be in the Black Hole, whence light and meaning and law and reason are banished and where there can be no way of knowing who he is, no sense of God's love and no answer to his, 'Why?'

That is the cost love is willing to bear. To be damned from God. To be fully identified with Sin and to be the Damned Thing on which God could not look. He would be repulsive to his Father and become the Great Reject from whom all the goodness of God would recoil. He would know a banishment to an area of reality – if reality it was – where no creature had gone before. That is what he took; and as 'Rabbi' Duncan reminded us, took 'lovingly'.[1] This is what the hymn-writer recalled with wonder:

That on the cross, my burden gladly bearing,
He bled and died, to take away my sin.

Thirdly, at the moment when the Saviour rose, took the towel and washed the disciples' feet, he knew that he came from God and was returning to God. He knew who he was, the very Son of God; and the foot-washing is the expression of this sense of identity. It is as if, knowing his own divinity, he wished to give it dramatic, definitive utterance: to do something 'matchless, godlike and divine'. How marvellous that the sign should be the washing of his disciples' feet! In that act, not in something overwhelming, Jesus discloses what it means to be the One from God. He shows that the impulse to service lies at the very heart of deity. God the Father serves the Incarnate Son. God the Son serves his sinful people. Is there not reason to trace the principle right back into the depths of the Trinity? God lives in a fellowship, a fellowship of service, where each person is for the other. Of course, there is no need. None is in want. None is deficient. But that is so only because each so fully serves the other. The Son is toward the Father (John 1:1). His whole being and strength and love move outwards, to the Other. That is why, in washing feet, the Lord is not only acting in full accordance with his hour, and in full accordance with his love, but in full accordance with his nature. He *is* love and it is the very nature of love to be for the Other.

'If I have washed your feet you also should wash one another's feet.' But is that the way it is? Are we a community of foot-washers?

Knowing that we are sons of God – that we, too, are in our own degree (2 Pet. 1:4) 'matchless, godlike and divine', do we express the glory of our position by stooping to the lowliest, least-acknowledged and least-rewarded task?

Peter doesn't understand, and makes his consternation plain in a series of inappropriate outbursts. Do *you* wash *my* feet! You shall never wash my feet! Not my feet only but also my hands and my head! He speaks for all of us who find God's way of salvation so inappropriate. A God who washes feet! A God who becomes incarnate, shares our sorrows and dies, being our sins. A God who justifies the ungodly and gives a free pardon to the chief of sinners: 'Lord, we have heard from many about this man, how much harm he has done!' A God who when he saves us doesn't do it at a stroke but leaves us struggling with indwelling sin and thorns in our flesh. We want a God whose feet we can wash and whom we can place in our debt so that we can walk into heaven with our heads high: self-made, self-washed, self-saved.

But what a marvellous thing Jesus says to him: 'What I am doing, you don't understand just now, but you will understand afterwards.'

How often have these words been quoted to comfort us in 'the storms of life'! These experiences seem so cruel, so undeserved, so spiritually sterile. But one day, we shall understand:

> God is His own interpreter,
> and he will make it plain.

That may be true. Indeed, it is true. But it has nothing to do with what is said here. It was the foot-washing the disciples didn't understand and that wasn't a trouble or a pain or a sorrow but a huge, utterly unmanageable blessing. It was a *good* and that, often, is what is so difficult to understand. Aren't there times when God is so sheerly good that it takes our breath away. Today, we are so conscious of the problem of evil: all the pain and suffering in the world make it so difficult to believe in God. But what of the problem of the Good? We stand in the midst of life, knowing what we deserve, and the Universe shows us a great kindness and our consciences say at once, 'This isn't right! You don't deserve this! How can there be a God in heaven?'

But Peter wasn't on that plane. His problem was not that he was overwhelmed

by the love exemplified in the foot-washing.
He just didn't understand it at all. He didn't
see it as love. And the same would be true of
the cross, where the love would shine even
more brightly. To Peter, it would simply be
Darkness. A Disaster.

How often is divine kindness mis-
construed. Had Peter known, how he would
have cherished and prolonged the foot-
washing. How much do we miss because,
'What I do thou knowest not now'!

6. THE CRUCIFIED GOD

Christ was crucified; and Christ was God. Jurgen Moltmann has ample warrant, therefore, for giving his book on the cross the title, *The Crucified God.*[1] Before there is a rush to buy it, however, we should warn readers that it is a fairly weighty specimen of academic theology. Furthermore, Moltmann could not satisfy Karl Barth as to his orthodoxy and can hardly expect, in the circumstances, to be endorsed by many of my readers. Indeed, some might think he were better left unmentioned in these pure and august pages. The trouble is, we owe him not only the title of this chapter but a good deal of theological stimulus besides, and it would be immoral to borrow without acknowledging our debt. Moltmann has clearly highlighted the paradoxical nature of the fact that God was crucified; insisted that it is not something we can just take in our stride; and drawn attention to some of its revolutionary implications for our theology, our individual Christian practice and our ecclesiastical ethos. The fact of the crucified God must be not only the foundation but the judge of our Christianity. The cross, said Luther, is the test of everything (*Crux probat omnia*).

But before looking at its implications for the church and for theology we must first of all look at the cross in itself. The sufferings it involved can be briefly summarised under four headings.

Physical suffering

First, our Lord suffered physically. His body, like our own, was severely limited in its powers of endurance and highly sensitive to pain. In common with other men he suffered, in that body, hunger, thirst, weariness and exhaustion. Beyond other men, he suffered the physical agony of Calvary: the whipping, the immolation, the many hours' suspension, fully conscious, upon the cross itself. These experiences were imprinted indelibly upon his memory, so that today not even the most excruciating pain is beyond the Saviour's personal understanding: 'He knoweth our frame; he remembereth that we are dust' (Ps. 103:14).

Emotional suffering

Secondly, our Lord suffered emotionally. He had an ordinary human psychology (sinfulness excepted). It would be morbid to overlook the fact that in that psychology he knew many hours of joy and contentment. Indeed, we could say that his sinless personality was so fully integrated that these were his basic and characteristic emotions. Yet he also knew the dark side of our psychology, not only occasionally, but habitually. He was 'the man of sorrows'. He was distressed by the spiritual hardness of those among whom he ministered, grieved by their opposition and pained by their misery. He wept in the presence of death, seeing it as an outrage: and he wept over Jerusalem, a great collective of sins and sorrows, doomed to destruction.

These dark emotions were intensified by the shadow of Calvary – a shadow which hung over him from the beginning of his ministry. As early as Mark 2:20, he speaks of a day when he will be violently taken away from his disciples. But the burden became particularly evident after Peter's confession at Caesarea Philippi: 'And they were in the way going up to Jerusalem; and Jesus went before them; and they were amazed; and as they followed, they were afraid.' These words speak of a solemn awesomeness in the demeanour of our Lord – one which filled the disciples with fear and foreboding.

These pent-up emotions erupt in Gethsemane. He is sore amazed. He is very heavy. He is exceeding sorrowful – 'unto death'. He throws himself on the ground in the intensity of his agony. The cause? His clear vision of what God's will for him involved: 'Father, if it be possible, let this cup pass from me.' The experience drains him – so much so that an angel has to be sent from heaven to strengthen him.

In these things, Christ still stands beside those who are emotionally overborne, finding their grief and bewilderment insupportable and likely to be fatal. Most of us, of course, enjoy so much of God's goodness that we should find it no great difficulty to 'make melody in our hearts and be thankful always and in all things' (Eph. 5:19f.) But there are some who are simply terrified by the unfolding will of God. Gethsemane is their reminder that the

Saviour can enter fully into their fear; as it is also a reminder that such fear is not necessarily something to be ashamed of.

Social suffering

Thirdly, our Lord suffered socially. Our starting-point here must be the recollection that Christ loved his neighbour as himself – not coldly and formally but warmly and affectionately – and naturally wanted that love reciprocated. It was not easy, therefore, to be isolated, to be condemned by the religious establishment, to be deemed an embarrassment by his family and to have the multitude calling for his blood. The treatment he received from his immediate disciples was even more painful. They were chosen precisely 'to be with him' (Mk. 3:14). In his humanness he needed their friendship. Yet one betrayed him, another denied him and all forsook him. He died entirely bereft of support, encouragement or appreciation, knowing that those who were closest to him thought only that he was letting them down.

Spiritual suffering

Fourthly, our Lord suffered spiritually. There are two dimensions to this. One is his exposure to Satan and the powers of hell which began with the threefold temptation early in his ministry. These temptations were repelled, but we should not assume that they were repelled easily. Significantly, we are told that his victory followed a time of fasting (Matt. 4:2). Luke tells us that after this the devil left him; but only 'for a season' (Lk. 4:13), which clearly suggests that the attack was soon renewed. It became particularly intense in Gethsemane, where Christ has to 'agonise' against the suggestion that he should put 'the cup' (the Father's will; or, the way of the cross) away from him. It was here, probably, that he resisted 'unto blood, striving against sin' (Heb. 12:4).

But Gethsemane was only the shadow of Calvary, where the Satanic attack culminates. He is behind Judas' betrayal (John 13:27), Peter's denial and the disciples' flight (Lk. 22:31). *He* is the pervertor of justice in the courts of Annas, Herod and Pilate. He is the instigator of the chant, 'Crucify! Crucify!' and of the taunt, 'He saved others. Himself he cannot save!' From what Scriptures and experience teach, we may well infer that he subjected the mind of the Lord to an unceasing bombardment of sinful suggestions, horrid blasphemies and despairing forebodings.

On a deeper level, the Lord's spiritual sufferings climaxed in the severance of fellowship with his Father, indicated in the cry of dereliction, 'My God, my God, why hast thou forsaken me?' We are tempted to add – 'Whatever these words may mean!' because here we have neither experience nor revelation to guide us. He was clearly bereft of all that was fitted to comfort him: for example, the assurance of God's love, the awareness of God's help and the certainty of a triumphant outcome. That fact that he cried, 'My God!' rather than the usual 'Father! (Abba)' suggests that he also suffered the loss of a sense of his own identity. The incarnation itself was sufficient to obscure the Lord's identity from the eyes of ordinary onlookers. The inability to say 'Abba!' suggests that at last the veil of (imputed) sin, ignominy and suffering was so impenetrable that his sonship was obscured even from himself: not necessarily in the sense that he doubted it but in the sense that it was not present as any consolation to his consciousness.

The fact of his feeling deserted does not mean, however, that at last the Lord is all on his own. God had promised to help his servant (Isa. 42:1) and that promise could not be broken. Even when most alone and most forsaken the Father who had sent him was with him (John 16:32). Or, if we may introduce the third Person of the trinity, the eternal Spirit supported him as he offered himself without spot to God (Heb. 9:14). Recondite and mysterious though the subject is, it is not altogether without analogy in our own spiritual lives. Just as Christ was being helped and upheld even when he felt forsaken, so God's grace may be supporting his people even when they feel spiritually desolate. Sadly, the converse is also true: God's help may be absent when Christians feel most confident of it.

The forsakenness of Christ has important implications for the doctrine of the trinity. It renders utterly inadmissible the Sabellian denial that Christ is a distinct person from God the Father. It is difficult enough for this heresy to live with the idea of the Word being *with* God (1 John 1:1). It is impossible for it to live with the idea of the Son being *forsaken* by God. How could one mode or aspect of a person be forsaken by another? or one phase of a personality cry to another, 'Why hast thou forsaken me?'

The relation between the Word being

forsaken by God and the Word being *with* God is an intriguing one. From eternity there was communion between the Father and the Son. The face of the One was toward the Other in an unclouded reciprocal love. On the cross the One who had been *with* God is forsaken by God: or, if we may use a variant reading of Hebrews 2:9 (*choris* instead of *chariti*), the One who was *with* God comes to be *without* God. He is outside. He is an unholy and accursed thing. It is against the brilliant background of former eminence and privilege that the contrasting darkness of the dereliction is silhouetted most clearly. But then the dereliction (being without God) is only an intermediate point on a road leading somewhere else. The One who was *with* God comes to be *without* God in order that *we* should be with God. The New Testament says so explicitly: 'He died to bring us to God' (1 Pet. 3:18). The Son of God does not return empty-handed from the far country. He brings with him 'a multitude which no man can number' (Rev. 7:9), born without God, deserving to remain without God, but now, through the Son's forsakenness, brought so close to God that he can meticulously wipe away every tear from their eyes (Rev. 7:17).

In the previous chapter we looked, very briefly, at the actual suffering involved for Christ in the fact that he became the crucified God. By far the most important question raised by these sufferings is, What did they achieve? And the full answer is, of course, that they achieved redemption. They constituted a sacrifice which expiated sin, propitiated God, destroyed the devil and redeemed the church. The primary concern of any doctrine of the cross must be to do justice to these central elements in our salvation.

Our objective in this article, however, is a very limited one. We come back to Luther's *Crux probat omnia*: the cross is the test of everything. This applies not only to our doctrine of salvation but also, as Moltmann has pointed out, to our doctrine of the Christian life and our doctrine of God.

The cross the test of our lifestyle

The key word so far as the Christian life is concerned is that spoken by Christ in Mark 8:34: 'Whosoever will come after me, let him deny himself, and take up his cross, and follow me.' This cross cannot be identified with 'crosses' – those pains, annoyances and frustrations which come to all men regardless of whether they are Christians or not. The cross we are asked to bear as disciples is not common to us with all men. It is the result of making the same kind of choices as Christ made and thus provoking the world to treat us exactly as it treated him.

This means, first of all, that we must identify with the deprived and the outcast. From eternity, Christ was with God. Had he remained there, he would never have been crucified. Instead, he chose to be with us, and for us. He identified fully with lost men, sharing their sufferings and making their cause, his cause. He became their spokesman, advocate and at last their scapegoat.

The step was not confined to identifying with man racially. He identified with particular victims of oppression: with the Jews, groaning under the burden of Roman imperialism; with the poor, weary under the yoke of the Pharisees; with social outcasts like tax-gatherers and prostitutes; and with racial minorities like the Samaritans and the Syro-Phoenicians.

More strikingly still, Christ identified with those who, morally and spiritually, were totally unlike himself. The ethical contrast between Christ and the woman taken in adultery is absolute. Even when he becomes her spokesman, he does not become like her. Nor does he condone her sin.

An authentic, cross-bearing church must similarly identify with the despised, the inarticulate, the helpless, the defenceless and the godless. But involvement must never become assimilation. When the church serves those whom man despises and whom God has forsaken, it must retain its own differentness. The light must shine at the heart of the darkness; but the darkness must not extinguish it.

The second implication of taking up the cross is that the church, in its prophetic ministry, cannot keep a low profile. At the moment, we are suffering from a gross surfeit of the wisdom that consists only in avoiding trouble. We are reluctant to speak out, terrified of giving offence and quite content to go on uttering platitudes within well-defined party lines. It was this mentality that allowed the church to pussy-foot its way through the Highland Clearances, the Robertson Smith case and the jingoism of the early days of the First World War. It was precisely because he refused to keep such a low profile that Christ was crucified. 'Jesus,' writes Moltmann, 'did not suffer passively from the world in which he lived but invited it against himself by his message and the life he lived.'[2] The cross did not simply happen to him. He provoked it by his own words and actions. His death itself was a priestly act. But he provoked it by his prophetic ministry and especially by his scathing denunciations of the self-appointed guardians of the law. His talk was, to say the least, 'careless'.

In its prophetic ministry today, the church must adopt an equally high profile and use equally careless language. We have no right to ignore the problems which lie at the heart of man's economic, moral and spiritual predicament. Nor have we any right to make the preservation of a formal peace our over-riding consideration. There can be no low profile on political heartlessness, institutional violence, Protestant bigotry, Romish intrigue or Gaelic intransigence. Where elders bind congregations to arrangements suited only to the conditions 100 years ago; where traditionalism masquerades as orthodoxy or heresy as theological creativity; where ministers so lose their zeal that they look only for 'easy charges' or 'peace in my time'; where a liberal establishment discriminates fiercely against evangelicals while at the same time boasting of its tolerance: these are not situations calling for a low profile but for high visibility and plain speech. The way of the cross means telling the church and the world what neither of them wants to hear. It means disregarding the advice of friends who counsel silence and even running the risk of having our own special circle gnashing their teeth.

Thirdly, taking up the cross means being willing to be nothing. For Christ, the cross was the result of his self-emptying (Phil. 2:7). He made himself nothing. He was willing to have his glory veiled and his identity obscured. He became so utterly *incognito* that there was nothing in his appearance, in his circumstances or even in his achievements to compel recognition. Things will be the same for an authentic church. The world knoweth us not (1 John 3:1). Our election is a great comfort to ourselves. But it cannot be used to compel human recognition or to protect us from human hostility.

Christ went further than merely foregoing recognition and acclaim, however. He became in the fullest and most public sense a servant. He did not sit in the place of honour with those who were being waited on but chose, instead, to stand with those who were doing the waiting (Mk. 10:45) and whose service was totally unappreciated. Indeed, men were scandalised both at the kind of service he rendered and at the way he rendered it. He could not even vindicate himself. He was in the right and he knew that he was in the right. But he allowed himself to be put in the wrong and to be seen only as condemned, outcast, despised and defeated. Not all suffering involves such rejection. Very often the sufferer is upheld by the knowledge that his suffering is acclaimed and appreciated and that although he is hated by his persecutors he is lauded by his peers. For Christ, it was far different. He suffered without admiration and without compassion.

For the church, this means an end to all imperialism. The moments when the world shouts *Hosannas* and scatters palm-branches in the path of the people of God (John 12:13) are to be rare and exceptional: and dubious. The normal attitude will be hatred, contempt and persecution. When the church finds herself sitting at the top table with the politicians, the academics, the sportsmen and the pop-stars, it is virtually certain that she has abandoned the way of the cross.

It is easy enough to see this imperialism in others and notably in the pretensions of the papacy. The claims to infallibility, universal primacy and temporal supremacy are glaring contradictions of the Christian ethos. It is much more important, however, to recognise the problem as it affects ourselves. The Disruption church in Scotland was born amid universal acclaim. Its leaders, as Hugh Miller pointed out, were 'some of the ablest and most eminent men that ever adorned the Church of Scotland'. A church born in such circumstances and led by such men expected (and got) the respect and even the adulation of the nation. They were part of the Scottish Victorian establishment, if not indeed its very creators. It is tempting to covet the same role and the same prestige for ourselves today. But our more immediate roots lie in the testimony borne by the 26 'Wee Frees' of 1900 – a pathetically small group of unknowns, rejected not only by the world but by the church of their day. Lord Balfour of Burleigh said that there was not a man among them 'of large ideas or of knowledge of affairs'.[3] Yet they were men of enormous courage and the photograph which shows them locked out of their own Assembly Hall is probably a more fitting symbol of a crucified church than D. O. Hill's famous painting of the Disruption.

The temptation to triumphalism is particularly acute for those of us who are in the ministry. It is all too easy to misconceive our role, seeing it as a juridical and authoritarian one rather than as a caring and pastoral one. We seek not so much to serve but to be recognised, supported and obeyed. We entertain expectations of revival which reflect only the hope of greater power and influence, and the longing for a day when the church will sit in the world's places of honour. The vision of church dominance of education and politics and the concern for a closer church-state partnership can all too easily become protests against the way of the cross. We have to keep on reminding ourselves that the church is in the community not to lord it over it but to serve it: and if the community fails to appreciate us, that is no sign that we are living in a particularly cloudy and dark day. It is only a sign that after the heady days of the 19th century, with their *Hosannas!* and palm-branches, things are now very much back to normal – back to what Christ meant them to be.

Caution

Two words of caution must be spoken, however, when we refer to the Christian life as the way of the cross.

First, the cross of Christ himself was utterly unique. We take up *our* cross, not his. Because he was the Son of God his cross was an outrage in a sense that ours can never be. Furthermore, it was unique in its (redemptive) effect and above all, in its content. He suffered the curse. He was put outside – to the far country. He was deprived of the one thing which could comfort the crucified – the sense of the presence of God. The summons to cross-bearing is not, for us, a summons to accursedness because the very reason for Christ suffering it was that we should be exempt.

Secondly, the cross must not be made the archetype or the excuse for our own weakness. The temptation is very strong. An impotent ministry, declining attendances, failed church extension – our self-pity can easily project these as 'our cross'. Before we know where we are, we are comforting ourselves with such thoughts as that Christ made no impact, that his attendances fell away and that people ignored what he said.

But these are only half truths. Christ's death does not belong to the same order of reality as our pastoral and evangelistic failure. His cross was the sign of his involvement whereas our failure is often due to our non-involvement. We fail because we refuse to run the risk of being crucified. Not only that. His cross was an instrument of victory. It destroyed Satan and put the Lord's enemies to an open shame. His weakness became the power of God. His foolish decision to be crucified became God's wisdom. His servitude – even his *servility* – became the ground of his lordship. His dying released the spiritual forces of the last days and the word of his cross became the saving power of God.

The sign of a crucified church is not failure but success. But the success cannot be defined in worldly terms, as if it meant prestige, recognition and acclaim. It means, instead, that the word which men hate to hear brings them salvation; and that the people men despise become the salt of the earth and the light of the world – without ceasing to be despised. When we pretend to be somebody, we are impotent. When we are willing to be nothing, God's grace is made perfect in our weakness.

The cross tests our doctrine of God

We can look only very briefly at the second area illuminated by the fact of the cross, namely, our doctrine of God. Theologians have traditionally regarded it as an axiom that God cannot suffer. The church in the West spoke of him as *impassibilis*. The church in the East spoke of him in terms of *apatheia*. The question is whether, in the light of the cross, we can continue to speak in this way.

There can be no doubt that in Christ a divine person suffered. It was the son of God who experienced hunger, thirst and weariness, was crucified, died and was buried. Even more, it was the Son of God who in the moment of his dereliction was denied divine support and comfort. But according to the doctrine of the impassibility of God, these experiences referred only to our Lord's human nature. God the Father did not suffer. Nor did the divine nature, which, to quote the Secession theologian, John Dick, is 'fixed, immovable and unaffected by external causes'.

There are some aspects of this doctrine which one can accept unhesitatingly. For example, God could not suffer physically because he has no body. Nor could God suffer any internal emotional disturbance or upheaval of the kind we experience as a result of unresolved mental conflicts and imperfect integration of our personalities. He cannot lose his composure or show symptoms of stress and agitation. Further, there cannot be in God any merely passive suffering – suffering of which he is only the victim without being also its Foreordainer and Controller. Suffering cannot 'come at' him – or, to use James's phrase, he cannot simply 'fall into' it (Jas. 1:2). He can only experience it if he takes it and goes towards it. For God, suffering can only be a form of action.

But even after these concessions, serious question marks remain against the doctrine of impassibility as traditionally formulated.

First, the idea that God is a passionless, emotionally immobile Being is totally unscriptural. The Bible reveals him as a God of wrath and jealousy. It also reveals him as One who has no pleasure in the death of the wicked (Ezek. 33:11) and therefore, by implication, as One who is grieved when human beings destroy themselves. The New Testament even describes the Holy Spirit specifically as capable of grief (Eph. 4:30). Similarly, God is revealed as One who is passionate in his love, loving the church as a husband loves his wife, extravagant in his devotion and tormented by her infidelities. These are all fundamentally important parts of the biblical portrait of God and quite irreconcilable with the view that he is emotionally inert.

Secondly, the idea that God is unaffected by occurrences outside himself is inconsistent with the divine pity. Pity means by definition that one is stirred by the spectacle of human misery, temporal and spiritual. God cannot pity and yet remain unmoved. Indeed, for God to remain unmoved would raise serious questions as to his morality. The pain and grief which we feel when confronted with inhumanity, deprivation and squalor must have its counterpart (and indeed its source) in the God whose image we bear.

Thirdly, the idea that God is impassive and apathetic is inconsistent with the cross (which is the test of everything). We cannot say that Christ is our greatest word about God and yet say that we do not mean the crucified Christ. Nor can we say that the crucified *Christ* is the image of God and yet say that the *cross* is only a word about his human nature. It is precisely the crucified Christ who is the revelation; and what he reveals, in being crucified, is God.

Consequently, when the New Testament appeals to the moral force and constraint of Calvary, it is on the involvement of God the Father that it frequently focuses. The cross is the expression of *his* love and of *his* pity (John 3:16, Rom. 8:32). *He* is the One whose conduct is the model of self-denial and cross-bearing. *He* is the One who bore the cost of redemption. Indeed, if he is so immobile and so passionless that Calvary cost him nothing, all talk of him must cease because our language about him is meaningless. If Calvary was painless for him, we are not made in his image and he does not love with our love. When Abraham offered Isaac, there was pain; when Jacob lost Joseph, there was pain; when David lost Absalom, there was pain. If things were different when God gave up his Son then either he does not love his Son or his love is so radically different from ours as to be meaningless. We cling therefore to the belief that not only did God the Son suffer crucifixion, but God the Father suffered the pain of delivering him up. The Father was as really bereft as the Son was forsaken: and the Father suffered the loss of the Son as really as the Son suffered the loss of the Father. The Father did not suffer what the Son suffered (He was not crucified). But he suffered seeing the Son suffering and the even greater (and quite unfathomable) agony of being the One who had to bruise and forsake him. He had to steel himself not to respond to the terrible cry from the far country, 'My God, my God, why hast thou forsaken me?'

Yet Calvary was not an isolated moment of pain or pity in the experience of God. Its roots lay in the primaeval and permanent concern of God for his creation. The cross does not inaugurate that concern. But it does show how deep and passionate it is, and how far God was prepared to go.

In the last analysis that concern is triune, shared equally by the Father, the Son and the Holy Spirit, as the history of the cross (involving the Father, the Son and the eternal Spirit) clearly testifies. The agony of each is different, yet equally real. And the resulting understanding of human grief is as much a reality for God the Father and God the Holy Spirit as it is for God the Son. The trinity is touched with the feeling of our infirmities.

7. WHY DID GOD SACRIFICE HIS SON?

Any discussion of the atonement must begin with the facts: the sufferings and death of Christ. His blood was shed. His soul departed. He became an inanimate corpse. Furthermore, all this happened in circumstances of particular solemnity: on a cross, the symbol of the divine curse; tormented by the forces of Hell, whose hour of power it was; deserted, in the hour of his greatest need, by God his Father. He cried; and God was not there. There was no voice of reassurance or encouragement; no sense of divine sonship; no possibility of saying, 'Abba! Father!'. There were no words of explanation. There was no promise of victory or deliverance. Instead, there was only that which caused him to tremble: the sight of a holy God and the knowledge of the sin which he bore and which, at last, he was (2 Cor. 5:21). He saw himself only as a condemned man, a man in the wrong. He was ruined. He was anathema. He was devoted to destruction. Of course he could not be destroyed. The glory of his person – who he was – would not allow that. Nor would the glory of his work. But he was not to know that. The veil was complete. He was not the Son. He was the Sinner: what Luther called 'the greatest sinner ever'.[1] His was a soul under unimaginable stress, almost overwhelmed, almost destroyed, almost disintegrating, surviving only by the resoluteness of his will and the ministry of his Spirit.

People speak of the Penal *Theory* of the atonement. It is no theory. It is a fact. He died, didn't He? And death is the wages of sin. Whatever happened on that cross, and whatever it means, there Jesus Christ was dealt with as a sinner. There as the Last Adam he experienced the penalty with which Jehovah God had long since threatened the First: 'The day you eat, you will surely die.'

Three facts
To see the full force of this we must remember three facts.

First *what* Christ was. He was utterly without sin. Not even his most malicious accusers could find evidence against him. This means that on that cross something appalling was happening: the only sinless man that ever was was being treated as the greatest sinner that ever was.

Secondly, *who* Christ was: the Son of God. As such he was uniquely beloved and precious. As such he was invulnerable, surely, to the terrors of law and of God. Yet there he hangs, in agony, almost demented, bearing all the marks of a criminal, a vicious, godless blasphemer, to whom the pious mothers of Israel might point as a warning to their own sons: 'That's what happens to evil men'. The Son of God was hell-bound.

Thirdly, who was behind it all? Who is giving the wages of sin to the sinless one? Who is sending God's Son to Hell? God himself! Time and again the Bible says it. It pleased Jehovah to bruise him (Isa. 53:10). He hath put him to grief. He made him sin (2 Cor. 5:21). He delivered him up for us all (Rom. 8:32). He *gave* him (John 3:16), putting his love for the world before his love for his Son. Behind the sacrifice of the cross there lies not only the priesthood of Christ but the priesthood of the eternal Father:

And when I see that God his Son not sparing
Gave him to die, I scarce can take it in;
That on that cross, my burden gladly bearing,
He bled and died, to take away my sin.

Immoral?

Men speak of the immorality of such a theory of the atonement. That is short-sighted. The real immorality lies in the facts. The Cross is immoral. There the innocent suffers: at God's hands. There God's Son is destroyed: at God's hands. Let's not sentimentalise it. This is not some 'green hill far away'. It is the scene of the greatest atrocity in history. Calvary is, quite literally, a shambles. God's Lamb is being slaughtered: on a garbage heap, outside the city, in darkness, by a brutal soldiery. And God is responsible.

Place some theories of the atonement in the light of this and they shrink. The problem, said Anselm long ago, is that men simply don't grasp the gravity of sin (*Nondum considerasti quantum ponderis sit peccatum*).[2] But is even that deep enough? The real problem is that we haven't grasped the moral gravity of the cross. Can we stand here, where God gave up his Son, and say: 'He did it to melt our hearts!' Can we stand here, where Christ was consumed by His Father's anger,

and say that all the atonement God asks for is
an adequate repentance? Put some ideas into
the crucible of facts – into the cry of
dereliction – into 'made sin' – and they shrivel
up.

It is not the evangelical doctrine of the
atonement that needs to be justified. It is
Calvary. What right had God to crucify his Son?
The cross itself needs redemption, because as
Donald Baillie put it, 'the crucifixion might well
seem to be the final *reductio ad absurdum* of the
belief that the world is governed by a gracious
providence.'[3]

The answer lies in Christ's relation with his
people. At one level we can describe it simply
in terms of *solidarity*. Christ came and stood
with us, sharing all the misery of our condition:
our creatureliness, our dependence, our
accountability, our frailty, our temptations, our
sufferings. He shared our curse. He died *with*
us.

But as Karl Barth pointed out, 'Even the
strongest "with us" is not enough to describe
what Jesus Christ is in relation to us'.[4] If he
merely dies *with* us, we die too. We perish
eternally. Is he, then, our *representative*? This
too, is true. He acted for us, as a priest
representing his people; as an advocate (1 John

2:1) representing his clients. But *on behalf of* is not enough. This advocate ends up in the dock, even on the gallows; this priest ends up on the altar, as a sacrifice. A sacrifice cannot be merely representative. It is substitutionary. No other word will do. The New Testament evidence for it is overwhelming. Christ was made sin for us (2 Cor. 5:21). He gave his life a ransom for many (Mark 10:45). He gave himself as a *substitutionary-ransom (antilutron)* for all (1 Tim. 2:6). He was made a curse for us (Gal. 3:13).

He died for sin (the only reason a man can die). But not for his own sin. He had none. He died for *our* sins (Gal. 1:4).

Without substitution, the death of Christ is unintelligible. That he died is beyond question. That death is the wages of sin is also, for the theologian, beyond question. Why then does the sword fall here? Why is there curse where there is no sin? 'The universe were one vast hell of suspense and horror,' wrote Hugh Martin, 'if God's wrath could alight elsewhere than where it is deserved'[5]. But if Christ is our substitute his death is right. He is in the sinner's place. He is brother, friend, husband, head and king to his people. He is one with them in the most profound and comprehensive sense: by nature, by Spirit, by covenant. In that union he contracts sin. He becomes his church. He inherits its debts. He assumes its guilt.

Without guilt, the cross remains a shambles. The justification of God's priesthood lies in the intimacy of Christ's union with his guilty people. This union was not only ontological and transformational (by the Spirit). It was also forensic: by substitution, imputation and covenant. This has been the historic doctrine of the church, in Scotland and beyond. 'Christ is innocent as concerning his own person,' wrote Martin Luther, 'and therefore he ought not to have been hanged. But he sustained the person of a sinner and of a thief; not of one, but of all sinners and thieves. He took all our sins upon him, and for them died on the cross.'

Expiation

Here is the vindication of God: the Crucified One was Sin. But, so understood, what did the cross achieve?

First of all, the cross had an effect on sin: it *expiated* it. The clearest statement of this is in Hebrews 2:17, which the A.V. wrongly translates, 'to make *reconciliation* for the sins of the people'. What the writer says is that

Christ made *expiation*. The roots of this idea
lie in the Hebrew *kipper*, to cover. The
sacrifice of Christ, the supreme act of
obedience, covers sin. Paul expresses it
succinctly in Romans 5:19: 'By the obedience
of the one man the many were made righteous
(just as by the disobedience of the one man
the many were made sinners).'

> My Saviour's obedience and blood
> Hide all my transgressions from view

That covering is total. There is absolutely no
condemnation to those who are in Christ
Jesus (Rom. 8:1).

Secondly, the cross had an effect on God.
This idea is dismissed in many theological
quarters. Some are so pre-occupied with the
subjective, man-ward effects of the atonement
that they see nothing else. Others allege that
God is unchanging and impassible and
therefore cannot be affected by anything
outside himself. Yet others stress that it is God
who takes the initiative in salvation, that there
is no need to earn his love and that therefore
the whole idea of a God-ward atonement is
sub-Christian.

Over against all such arguments stands the
inescapable insistence of scripture that the

primary movement of atonement and sacrifice is heaven-ward. Christ 'offered himself without spot to God' (Heb. 9:14). Anselm spoke of this God-ward movement as a *satisfaction* and both the Scots Confession (Chapter XV) and the Westminster Standards followed suit: Christ offered himself a sacrifice 'to *satisfy* divine justice', says the Shorter Catechism (Answer 25). By using this term orthodoxy was saying that Christ did enough to meet the requirements of God. He paid all our debts. As to why justice had to be satisfied, the only possible answer is, Because it's there. God cannot act unjustly, least of all in the process of justification and atonement. It must become *right* to forgive.

The term *satisfaction*, however, is not biblical. The New Testament uses two other words: *reconciliation* and *propitiation*.

So far as reconciliation is concerned, scripture clearly emphasises that it is God himself who takes the initiative (2 Cor. 5:18ff.). But this is not inconsistent with God also being the one who is reconciled. All his saving activity is rooted in love and this love is completely unconditional and unearned. It is not the function of the atonement to make God love us. His love is already there, a sheer

sovereign mercy, providing the atonement.
But even as such it does not proceed directly
to reconciliation. The background to
atonement is that God simultaneously loves
and condemns and that love proceeds to
reconciliation only by removing the grounds
of the condemnation. This means that
between love and reconciliation there are two
momentous steps: Christ is made sin; and
because of that we are made righteous (2 Cor.
5:21). It is only as such – as righteous – that
God is reconciled to us. He may love us
simply as sinners, but he is reconciled to us
only as those whose sin has been condemned
in the flesh of Jesus Christ (Rom. 8:3). It is
totally illegitimate to use 2 Corinthians 5:18ff.
as proof of God's loving initiative without
giving equal emphasis to the fact that
according to the very same passage our debts
have been cancelled only because they have
been transferred to Christ (2 Cor. 5:19). The
reconciliation takes place not in the depths
of the trinity and not in the hearts of men
but on the timber of Calvary.

Propitiation

The other word used by the New Testament
to define the God-ward effect of the

atonement is *propitiation*. The Greek word is the same as the one which (in the form of a verb) we have already seen in Hebrews 2:17. There it has to be translated *expiate*, because it refers to *sins* and you cannot *propitiate* sins; you *expiate* them. C. H. Dodd argued that in biblical Greek this word never means to *propitiate*: that it always means to expiate.[6] Dodd's linguistic arguments were subjected to rigorous review by Leon Morris and Roger Nicole, who showed that in both the Septuagint and classical Greek this word-group invariably suggested propitiation and appeasement.[7] But Dodd's case was only partially linguistic. His main argument was theological: there was no place in Christianity for the idea of an angry deity. Indeed, such a notion was utterly pagan. Presumably Dodd was drawing a distinction here between *Christian* and *biblical*, because the God of the Bible is indubitably angry. That anger is not capricious or egotistical or irrational or malevolent. The God and Father of our Lord Jesus Christ doesn't go into moods. To that extent a distinction has to be drawn between pagan notions and Christian ones. But the anger is real enough nonetheless. Without it, huge tracts of scripture become unintelligible:

the expulsion from Eden, the Deluge, the destruction of Sodom and Gomorrah, the Exile, the death of Ananias and Sapphira. In fact, anger against sin is part of the very definition of a moral being. Biblical monotheism would not be *ethical* monotheism if it were indifferent to inhumanity and ungodliness.

When early Christian preachers and writers used the word *hilaskesthai* they were using a word which to both Jews and Greeks suggested placating someone who was angry. We cannot escape from this fundamental idea even by limiting the translation of *hilasmos* to expiation. What is the point of expiation but to cover sin from the sight of God? Why need it be covered except that if not covered it will call forth God's holy response? By expiating sin the obedience of Christ propitiates God. The one notion is inseparable from the other.

Redemption

Thirdly, the effect on sinners: it *redeems* them. In the secular world this word referred to the emancipation of slaves and the ransoming of prisoners-of-war. It carries the same meaning in scripture. Christ's death liberates. It secures freedom. This freedom is many-sided: freedom from the curse of the law (death in the full range of its meaning); freedom from the power of sin (Titus 2:14); freedom from the authority of the Darkness (Col. 1:13); and freedom from 'the doctrines and commandments of men'.[8] The emphasis the New Testament places on this is most striking (1 Pet. 1:18, Gal. 5:1). Whenever we are tempted to surrender our liberty of conscience, let us remember that Christ died to make us free. What bold words Luther used in his tract, *The Freedom of a Christian*: 'Use your freedom constantly and consistently in the sight of and despite the tyrants and the stubborn so that they also may learn that they are impious, that their laws are of no avail for righteousness, and that they had no right to set them up'![9] Yet the freedom is not absolute. We are not only redeemed from sin. We are redeemed *to God*. We are his peculiar property (Titus 2:14). We are bought with a price (1 Cor. 6:20).

This last statement reminds us that redemption always implies cost. Grace is extravagant and free. But it is not cheap. We are free only because Christ has paid the ransom (with his blood, Mark 10:45, 1 Tim.

2:6, 1 Pet. 1:19). He has secured our immunity from the curse by enduring the curse himself (Gal. 3:13). God has bought us with his own blood (Acts 20:28).

There is no way that this doctrine can be tied up in a neat package. God demands the price; but yet, equally, God *pays* the price, bearing within himself the whole cost of our forgiveness, our transformation and our freedom. Why did such a price have to be paid? Because of the very nature of God. Even in forgiveness he condones nothing. If the death of Christ was anything less than absolutely necessary it was vanity (Gal. 2:21); and if *that* was vanity all is vanity. 'What kind of love,' wrote John Owen in his *Dissertation on Divine Justice*, 'can that be which God hath shown, in doing what there was no occasion for him to do? ... I cannot see but that Christ has died in vain on the supposition that God could pardon sins without the intervention of a ransom, justice not demanding their punishment'.[10]

The redemption is commensurate with the price. We are as free as the blood of Christ deserves, precious to God beyond our wildest imaginings because for each one of us he paid, literally, a King's ransom. At last, we cost him himself.

Victory

Finally, the effect of the cross on the forces of darkness. It *conquered* them. This aspect of biblical teaching suffered centuries of relative neglect until the publication of Gustaf Aulen's *Christus Victor* in 1931.[11] Aulen protested that 'the work of Christ is first and foremost a victory over the powers which hold mankind in bondage: sin, death and the devil.' This neglect was all the more inexcusable in that the very first announcement of the gospel striked precisely the note of victory: The Seed of the Woman will bruise the serpent's head (Gen. 3:15). The theme also dominates the great Servant Song of Isaiah (52:13–53:12), which begins by affirming his exaltation and concludes with the promise, 'I will divide the spoil with the strong'. In the New Testament, Christ destroys the one who had the power of death, the devil (Heb. 2:14); he spoils principalities and powers, triumphing over them by the cross (Col. 2:15); he conquers death (1 Cor. 15:26).

How did he achieve his victory? By expiating sin. From this point of view, Aulen's *first and foremost* is wrong. First and foremost the cross is an expiation. Only by being such can it be a victory. By atoning for sin it robs Satan of his authority. The death which wipes out the sentence is the deathblow of Satan's kingdom. 'Those nails which pierced Christ,' wrote Thomas Crawford (commenting on Colossians 2:14), 'pierced also the sentence of doom'.[12] The priestly act of self-sacrifice is simultaneously the kingly act which destroys death and routs hell. The marvel is that this was achieved precisely through his weakness. In the words of Hugh Martin, 'His cross was the instrument which, in the lowest ebb of his human strength, he wielded with Almightiness, through the Eternal Spirit, as the weapon of his warfare and the means of his victory'.[13]

The upshot is that Christ is the Alpha and Omega, the Lord of history. The slaughtered Lamb is in the midst of the throne: the world will go his way, not the devil's. In the Garden, the serpent deposed Man. On the cross Christ restores him: 'thou hast put all things in subjection under his feet' (Heb. 2:8). He reigns, as Last Adam and Son of Man, over the age to come; and we shall reign with Him, pursuing as restored princes the great Creation Mandates to subdue, conserve and develop. The harmonies of the original order will be restored in him and the whole creation rejoice in the liberty of the glory of the sons of God (Rom. 8:21).

Christ reigns by the cross. But he also reigns for the cross, his sovereignty linked inseparably to Mission: 'I reign; you go!' (Matt. 28:18f.). At immeasurable personal cost he made himself a propitiation for the sins of the world. Now, from his throne, he dispenses the life which his sacrifice secured.

8. JESUS AND THE RESURRECTION

The resurrection of Christ has figured prominently in recent theological discussion, largely as a result of the headline-catching statements of David Jenkins, the Bishop of Durham. For the most part, however, attention has focused on the mere fact: did the resurrection really happen or not? Was it something to which early Christian faith was a response? Or something which that faith created? Very little attention has been given in the meantime to what the resurrection actually means. Yet even the most cursory examination shows that the resurrection is central to the New Testament. It is the foundation of the gospel and provides the only standpoint from which we can see the rest of the truth in proper perspective.

The Person of Christ

First of all, the resurrection profoundly affects the person of Christ. This is not simply to say that it determines *our perception* of him, true though that is: we could not see him as Lord, Messiah or Son of God if he were not risen. It is to say that the resurrection affects Christ as he is in himself. It means, for example, that in his present state he possesses a full humanity. He has not returned to his pre-existent state of being only divine. Nor does he exist now only in some disembodied state. The incarnation (the *en-manning* of the Son) is permanent. He is still man: and the manhood he now possesses is physical as well as spiritual. Yet it is not in the state in which it was before his death. It is glorified (Jn 17:1). The risen Christ has new might and majesty. His humanity, once so vulnerable, is now inviolable. And he is no longer the Man of Sorrows. It is true of himself before it is true of his people that God wipes away all tears from his eyes (Rev. 7:17).

On the other hand there is continuity between the pre-resurrection and post-resurrection Christ. While we may agree with Pannenburg that the transformation of his body was so radical that nothing remained unchanged,[1] we must also insist that it was the Lord's earthly body which experienced the change. It is probably inappropriate to describe this body as 'flesh and blood'. Flesh and blood cannot inherit the kingdom of God (1 Cor. 15:50). Man as *flesh* cannot be raised. But man as *body* can and the body is by definition material. It is what gives man his affinity with his physical environment. The body of the First Adam was 'dust of the earth'. In the Last Adam that body is transfigured. But it is transfigured dust. 'The dust of the earth,' said 'Rabbi' Duncan, 'is an integral part of us. The dust of the earth is on the throne of the Majesty on High.'[2] In the Book of Revelation even the marks of his crucifixion remain on the ascended Christ (Rev. 5:6).

What is the relation between the resurrection and the divine sonship of Christ? It was certainly not the point at which he *became* the Son of God. He is sent into the world as Son (Rom. 8:3, Gal 4:4). Indeed it is the pre-existent sonship which gives point to such passages as John 3:16 and Romans 8:32. The whole emphasis of these statements falls upon the cost of our salvation to God the Father: and there was cost precisely because at the moment of Calvary, God was already

Father and Christ was already Son. They would lose all their force if Christ only became Son at the resurrection.

Yet the Authorised Version's translation of Romans 1:3 is mistaken: '*declared* to be the Son of God with power by the resurrection from the dead'. *Declared* is too weak. The usual meaning of the word used here is *to delimit*. There is no example either in the New Testament or in earlier literature of its meaning *to declare*. In Luke 22:22 it means *to determine*. 'The Son of Man goes as it was determined.' In Hebrews 4:7 it means *to limit*: 'Again he limits a certain day.' It is unacceptable to impose a novel meaning on the word in Romans 1:3. We must take it at its face value. Christ was *appointed* Son of God with power by the resurrection.

What is being said, however, is not that he was appointed Son of God, but that he was appointed Son of God *with power*. The contrast is not between a time when he was Son of God and a time when he was not Son of God, but between a time when he was the weak and humiliated Son of God and a time when he became the Son of God in full majesty and authority. It marks the end of his poverty and self-emptying. But that poverty was itself preceded by riches (2 Cor. 8:9) and the self-emptying was preceded by equality with God (Phil. 2:6). These considerations make it impossible to speak of the resurrection as an *adoption*. But it *was* a coronation: 'He was crowned with glory and honour because he had suffered death' (Heb. 2:9).

The Work of Christ

The resurrection was no less significant for the work of Christ. Protestant theology has rightly emphasised the *finished* work of Christ, but crucially important though this is we must not lose the balance of Scripture. Christ's post-resurrection existence is not one of idleness. The risen Jesus is seen *standing* on the right hand of God (Acts 7:55), a symbol of the fact that the interval between the resurrection and the second coming is filled with redemptive activity.

This again is already clear in John 17:2, where Jesus directly links the conferral of authority to his continuing work as Saviour: 'Thou hast given him power over all flesh, that he should give eternal life to as many as thou hast given him.' This is reinforced by the whole perspective of the Book of Acts, the story of what Jesus continued to do and to teach. It is the risen Lord who pours forth his Spirit at Pentecost (Acts 2:33), apprehends Saul on the road to Damascus, opens the heart of Lydia, and directs apostles in the conduct of their mission (Acts 17:9).

There is no room in the New Testament for the idea that Christ has stopped working, and Protestant theology grasped this firmly: 'Christ, as our Redeemer, executeth the offices of a prophet, of a priest, and of a king, both in his estate of humiliation *and exaltation*' (The Shorter Catechism, Answer 23).

It is the resurrection, obviously, which makes this resumption of his work possible and it affects all three aspects of his ministry as Prophet, Priest and King. The priestly work of intercession, for example, is specifically grounded in the fact that 'he ever liveth' (Heb. 7:25). It is also an intercession which takes place at 'the right hand of God'. It belongs to the resurrection state and partakes of the authority proper to that state. This is why, for example, in John 17:24, Christ says, not 'I *pray* that those whom thou hast given me be with me where I am' but '*I will*'. The intercession itself is imperious because it takes place within the exaltation.

So far as his work as prophet is concerned, the disciples fully expected that they would lose his teaching ministry if his earthly presence were withdrawn. When he announced that he was in fact leaving them, sorrow filled their hearts (John 16:6). But the outcome was entirely different. The risen Lord continued to teach his church. He was, for example, the real source of the apostles' teaching, as Paul makes plain in 1 Corinthians 11:23, 'I received from the Lord that which also I delivered to you.' He makes a similar claim in Galatians 1:12: 'I did not receive my gospel from man, neither was I taught it but by revelation from Jesus Christ.' The result was that in the apostolic teaching we have 'the mind of Christ' (1 Cor. 2:16) and 'the commandments of the Lord' (1 Cor. 14:37). But it was not only a matter of revelation. Christ was also the One who gave the insight and open-mindedness necessary to receive the Christian message. It is very interesting, for example, that it was *the Lord* who opened Lydia's heart (Acts 16:14). The strictly revelatory aspect of Christ's work as prophet finished with the ministry of the apostles. But the work of *illuminating* still continues. He could be neither Revealer nor Illuminator if he were not risen.

Enhancement of knowledge

We saw that the Lord's intercession was exalted. Is it possible to speak of his prophetic ministry in the same terms? In particular, did the resurrection bring significant enhancement of his knowledge? The idea is by no means a novel one. For example, John Calvin, in his commentary on Mark 13:32, suggests that after his resurrection Christ received that knowledge of the timing of his Second Advent which was withheld from him during his life on earth.[3]

It is hardly possible to answer this question fully without a thorough examination of the sources of the Mediator's theological insight. But two pointers are available to us. One is the fact that during his earthly life Christ's knowledge was certainly not static. This is implied in the fact that he had a true human nature. Human knowledge is never static. But it is also explicitly stated that Jesus grew in wisdom (Luke 2:52). The second consideration is what happens to ourselves at death. Our knowledge is dramatically

increased. We see God face to face and come
to know even as we are known (1 Cor. 13:12).

There is no reason to assume that the
Lord's intellectual development ceased with
his death or that he differs from his people in
not receiving greater understanding when he
enters into the presence of his Father. The
knowledge possessed by his human mind was
obviously limited during his days on earth.
We must therefore believe either that it
remained fixed at the level it had attained by
the time he died or that it continued to
advance after his resurrection. The latter is
far more likely. His knowledge, no less than
his body, was glorified. This is not a case
simply of understanding the Father better. It
is also a case of understanding himself better.
His own glory and the meaning of his own
work become clearer and it is out of that
enhanced, exalted understanding of himself
that he ministers prophetically to his people.

When it comes to the kingship, we must
again guard against the idea that it began with
the resurrection. Christ is already *Lord* not
only in his pre-existence but even in his
humiliation. In him the King (and the
Kingdom) comes: 'What kind of man is this,

that even the winds and the seas obey him!'
(Matt. 8:27).

Post-resurrection sovereignty

What difference, then, did the resurrection
make?

First of all, the post-resurrection
sovereignty differs in its range. Up to the
resurrection, the mediatorial dominion of the
Son was limited to Israel. He was 'King in
Jeshurun' (Deut. 33:5). Now the nations are
given to him as his inheritance and the
uttermost parts of the earth as his possession
(Ps. 2:8). He has *all* the authority in heaven
and in earth (Matt. 28:18). This authority is
closely linked with world mission. The
evangelisation of every nation is only possible
because Christ's resurrection dominion
extends over the whole world; and evangelism
itself is the proclamation to every creature of
the good news that Christ is his Lord and that
he will have all men to be saved (1 Tim. 2:4).

The post-resurrection sovereignty also
differs in its close relation to the ministry of
the Spirit: so much so, in fact, that John can
even say that before Jesus was glorified 'the
Spirit was not yet' (John 7:39). In God's order,
the mission of the Comforter did not depend

only on the death of Christ but also on his resurrection and ascension: 'It is expedient for you that I go away: for if I do not go away, the Comforter will not come to you; but if I depart I will send him to you' (John 16:7). It is through his Spirit that Christ leads his people and governs the world.

But the most important difference is this: the post-resurrection sovereignty is modified and enriched by all the experiences of the Lord's incarnate life. In its pre-resurrection phase the sovereignty had all the advantages of his love, pity and omniscience. It still retains these but it is now enhanced by his involvement in the common lot of men during his earthly ministry. Even for God, the only way to gain compassion is by experience. Today, the memories of Nazareth and Cana, of poverty and pain, of temptation and suffering, of Gethsemane and Calvary, are imprinted indelibly on the Lord's memory and profoundly influence the way he runs his administration. It is as the Lamb who bore the sin of the world that he now sits on the throne (Rev. 5:6). He remembers that we are dust and knows our humanness from the inside. He can say, as he observes us, 'I know exactly how that woman feels!'

And because he himself lived on the outer
limbs of human endurance he can ensure that
we shall not be tested above what we are able
to bear.

9. DID PAUL CALL JESUS GOD?

According to the late C. H. Dodd, although Paul ascribes to Christ functions and dignities which clearly imply his deity, he pointedly avoids calling him *God.*[1] Dodd is not alone in this opinion. It is shared by Frances Young, one of the contributors to *The Myth of God Incarnate,* and by C. Anderson Scott, who regards it as quite improbable that one in whom the monotheistic faith of Judaism was as deeply ingrained as it was in Paul could have taken so tremendous a step.[2] Bultmann, curiously, is more cautious, at least to the extent of conceding that Jesus may possibly be called God in 2 Thessalonians 1:12 (an interpretation rejected even by the most conservative scholars).[3]

The issue

It is important to be clear as to the precise point at issue. The dispute relates only to the usage of Paul. It is not denied that other New

Testament writers refer to Jesus as God. In
Hebrews 1:8, for example, the language of
Psalm 45:6 is applied unreservedly to Christ,
'Thy throne, O God, is for ever and ever'.
The same identification appears in 2 Peter 1:1,
where the correct translation almost certainly
is, 'through the righteousness of our great
God and Saviour, Jesus Christ'. It appears
even more clearly in John, who places his
whole Gospel within the framework of two
great assertions of the explicit deity of the
Saviour – the opening statement which
declares that 'the Word was God,' and the
confession of Thomas, 'My Lord and my
God!' The former of these statements
indicates not only John's view of the dignity
of Christ but also the splendid profundity of
his own insight. By omitting the definite
article before God *(theos)* John is not (as
Jehovah's Witnesses and others claim)
reducing his statement to the impossible level
of 'the Word was a god'. He is avoiding a form
of language which would have meant either
'the Word was the Father' or 'the Word was
the godhead'. Both of these propositions
would have been erroneous. John's problem
was that he had to assert the deity of the Son
without prejudice to the deity of the Father

and he does this, negatively, by omitting the article and, positively, by going on to state, 'The Word was with God'. The Word was not the Father. Nor was the Word the only Person of the godhead. The Word was God with God.

There is no doubt, then, that the New Testament calls Jesus God. The only question is whether Paul does so. Even here, however, the problem must be carefully defined. We are not asking whether Paul believed unreservedly in the deity of Jesus because this is scarcely disputed. For example, the statement in Philippians 2:6 that Christ was in the form *(morphe)* of God is as forcible an expression of our Lord's divinity as anything we find in John. In classical Greek, *morphe* meant *the sum total of essential characteristics*. The form was what constituted a thing the precise thing that it was. To say, then, that Christ was in the form of God was tantamount to saying that he possessed all the essential qualities of deity.

More important than the classical meaning, however, is the way *morphe* is used in the Septuagint, the most important Greek version of the Old Testament. It is especially interesting that here, *morphe* is synonymous with *doxa* (glory), since both are used to translate the Hebrew word for *image*. To say, therefore, that Christ possesses the form of God is equal to saying that he possesses the glory of God. Paul is thus following John who declared that in Christ they beheld the glory of the only-begotten. James speaks of Christ as *the glory*, absolutely (James 2:1. The words in italics in the AV are not part of the original). To see the full significance of this we must recall the status of the glory of God in the Old Testament. It is something inseparable from God himself: 'I am Jehovah: this is my name: and my glory will I not give to another' (Is. 42:8). It is in this sublime and incommunicable sense that Christ is the glory of God. We must not forget, however, that in Christ the glory of God is not only revealed but also re-interpreted.. It takes the form of a servant (Phil. 2:7) and becomes synonymous with grace and truth (John 1:14).

Purchased with His own blood

Even if it could be shown, then, that Paul never calls Jesus *God,* this would not in any way affect our confidence as to the deity of our Lord since that doctrine is clearly asserted in so many other different ways. It would be foolish, however, to surrender without good reason any part of the New Testament witness to the glory of Christ and there are at least three passages in Paul's writings where the designation *God* appears to be applied to him. Unfortunately, all of them contain difficulties which need to be carefully unravelled.

Acts 20:28 is typical. In the Authorised Version it reads, 'Take heed...to feed the church of God, which he hath purchased with his own blood.' There is some doubt, however, as to the phrase 'the church of God'. Many manuscripts have the reading 'the church of *the Lord*', and on textual evidence alone it is very difficult to be sure exactly what the Apostle said. As B. B. Warfield points out,[4] the best uncial manuscripts are for *God*, the best miniscule manuscripts are for *Lord* and the most witnesses are for *the church of the Lord and of God*, running the two readings together. On balance, however, the evidence favours reading *God*, which is supported by the two great codices, Vaticanus and Sinaiticus, and also by the Latin Vulgate. This is reinforced by the consideration that the passage contains an evident allusion to Psalm 74:1, 2, 'O God... remember thy congregation (church) which thou hast purchased of old.'

Here the church is clearly conceived of as the church of God. Furthermore, it is easier to envisage a scribe changing *God* to *Lord* than to envisage him doing the opposite. Not only would the phrase 'the church of the Lord' be thoroughly familiar to him as the Old Testament designation of the people of God, but there would have been a very real aversion to the concept of the blood of God implied in the other reading. It would be resented by those like the Arians who denied the deity of Christ, by those others (the anti-patripassians) who feared the doctrine that it was the Father who suffered, and again by ordinary orthodox believers offended by the sharp contrast implied in *the blood of God* (as any preacher who has used the phrase in the pulpit will know). It is perfectly understandable that some should seek to soften the paradox by substituting *Lord*.

Scholars have also disagreed as to the phrase 'his own blood', some suggesting that this is a mistranslation and that the correct rendering is 'the blood of his own'. It is clear from the papyri that the phrase 'his own' was often used as a term of endearment, equivalent to 'beloved' or to the great phrase of Colossians 1:13, 'the son of his love', and F.

F. Bruce, for example, thinks that this is what we have in Acts 20:28.[5] The traditional translation, however, is equally tenable grammatically and is only suspect for the dogmatic reason already noted, namely, that it implied the concept of the blood of God. This phrase certainly needs to be carefully safeguarded but in the light of the doctrine of the Trinity and the New Testament facts which underlie it, it is perfectly acceptable. It is as valid (and as dangerous) as the concept of Mary as the bearer of God (*theotokos*) sanctioned by the Council of Chalcedon. Christ was a divine Person and that Person was the subject of all his experiences and actions. What he did, God did. What he suffered, God suffered. His church was God's church. His body was God's body. His blood was God's blood. Once we recognise that it was the Person who became incarnate who also died, the main objections to the traditional interpretation of Acts 20:28 are removed and the passage can be seen for what it is: a charge in which Paul rests the solemnity of our pastoral responsibility on two great facts — first that the church is the church of God and, secondly, that it was purchased with his blood.

God over all

There are at least two other places where Paul seems to call Jesus God, but space will allow only a brief reference to them. The first is Romans 9:5, 'Whose are the fathers, and of whom as concerning the flesh Christ came, who is over all, God blessed for ever.' The problem here is that we cannot be certain how the passage should be punctuated (there would have been no punctuation-marks in the original). The Revised Standard Version follows a considerable body of modern scholarship in adopting the form: 'to them belong the patriarchs, and of their race, according to the flesh, is the Christ. God who is over all be blessed for ever.' This effectively distinguishes Christ from God. Nothing in the Apostle's language, however, requires us to abandon the traditional translation – indeed, Cullmann comments that the RSV rendering 'is hardly the one suggested by a philological and material consideration of the context'.[6]

The other passage is Titus 2:13 which in the AV reads, 'Looking for that blessed hope, and the glorious appearing of the great God and our Saviour, Jesus Christ.' There is no doubt, however, but that this is grammatically (and theologically) untenable and that the RSV is correct in reading, 'the appearing of the glory of our great God and Saviour, Jesus Christ'. Apart from everything else it is Christ exclusively and not God the Father whose second coming constitutes the blessed hope. The problem here is not whether the passage calls Jesus *God* (which it certainly does) but whether it was written by Paul or by some anonymous writer making (unscrupulous) use of his name. We cannot discuss that question adequately here: nor would we like to dismiss it contemptuously. But it is difficult to believe that any of Paul's associates would have used his name to impose a bogus rule of faith and practice on the church while at the same time invoking God as a witness to his own seriousness and integrity (2 Tim. 4:1).

Why only three passages?

Considering Paul's evident conviction of the deity of his Saviour, however, it seems very strange that he should refer to him as God so infrequently. Part of the reason, undoubtedly, is that *God* was already in Paul's thinking the proper name of another divine person, God the Father. In such passages as Romans 8:3; 8:29-32, *God* is the one who sends and gives his Son and predestinates, calls, justifies and glorifies his people. This rule may occasionally be broken and the title applied to the Son. But such infringements are infrequent because of the need to avoid confusing what were to Paul two distinct persons. To him, Christ was undoubtedly divine, but he was not God the Father. The Father did not become incarnate or suffer or die. On the contrary, it was precisely and specifically God the Son who appeared for our salvation.

The other – and more weighty – part of the explanation of Paul's reserve is that he had an alternative designation for Christ which expressed fully and adequately all that he believed as to the divine glory of his Saviour. In at least 130 passages he speaks of him as *Lord*, a title which in Paul's day carried momentous overtones. On one level, it was a counter to the claim that Caesar was Lord. There was another Emperor to whom men owed a more basic and indeed an overriding allegiance; by whom in fact the powers that be were appointed and whom, more than any man, Christians were bound to obey.

On another level, the designation LORD related Jesus to the pagan deities. There were gods many and lords many, and the immediate Gentile understanding of Paul's message would have been that he was placing *his* lord in the category of beings to whom one offered religious veneration. Among such beings, however, Christ was not an equal. It might well be true that there were gods many and lords many but to Paul there was 'but one Lord, Jesus Christ, by whom are all things and we by him' (1 Cor. 8:6).

Above all, the designation *Lord* related Christ in the most intimate way to the God of the Old Testament. The Septuagint had resolved the problem of finding an equivalent for *Jehovah* by using the word *Kurios (Lord)*. Consequently, to Greek-speaking Jews in the first century, *the Lord* was Jehovah, and to say that Jesus was Lord was to make the greatest possible claim. It was to assert that he was equal with God. It is clear that Paul was fully conscious of what he was implying because in Philippians 2:9 he speaks of Christ as possessing *the name which is above every name*. Jesus was Jehovah and no higher name was conceivable. It represented the highest pinnacle of divine eminence. All that remained was that to him every knee should bow and every tongue should swear.

10. TO LIVE IS CHRIST

In many ways, General Assemblies are poor reflections of the life of the churches. Much of what they deal with is routine administration; and much is controversial and distasteful. It is only too easy for the press, therefore, to extrapolate the trivial and the sectarian and make us all look ridiculous.

But behind the Assemblies, there lies something infinitely more important – a year's ministry, expounding the Scriptures, evangelising those outside the church, and caring for the sick, the bereaved and the elderly. For most Christian workers – I do not speak for myself – the financial rewards for such ministry are meagre, or nil. Today, in addition, the encouragements are few. It is often an uphill task and a very lonely one.

What then, makes people do it? What motivates them? And what sustains them? The answer is given by the apostle Paul, in his letter to the church at Philippi: 'For me, to live is Christ'.

We in the Free Church claim no monopoly in this attitude. It underlies all Christian discipleship and that, thankfully, is not confined to any one denomination. But precisely by seeing ourselves as only one tiny element in a worldwide church we are recognising that not all Christians share our view of what discipleship means. Bearing that in mind then, we may ask – forgivably, I hope – 'What is the meaning for us as Free Churchmen of this great statement that life is Christ'.

Submitting our intellect

It means, first of all, the submission of our intellects to Christ. We are disciples or pupils and he is our infallible teacher – infallible because he is divine and because even in his humanness he was fully controlled by the Holy Spirit. It is inconceivable to us that disciples should take it upon themselves to differ from their Master's pronouncements on fundamental matters of faith and life.

The practical implications of this are momentous. I believe, for example, in the inerrancy of the Bible. Why? Not because I am unaware of current trends in Biblical studies or even because I can vindicate the

Bible against all the objections that may be adduced by historians, scientists and literary critics. My belief in inerrancy arises from loyalty to Christ. He said, 'The Scripture cannot be broken'. This position – the fundamentalist position, if you wish – is not bibliolatry. It is Christolatry. It is an act of devotion to the One we regard as a teacher sent by God.

The same logic lies behind our belief in Hell. By some curious quirk, this doctrine has come to be regarded as something quite eccentric to the Christian faith. Now of course it can be, and often is, preached badly. It may be too prominent in the preacher's message; the exposition may owe more to imagination – or to Milton and Dante – than to the New Testament; it may be preached without tenderness or love or pity. But none of this should obscure one vital fact: of all the great teachers we meet in the Bible, none speaks more often or more solemnly of Hell than Christ himself. He is the One who speaks of the broad road to destruction, of the place of outer darkness, and of a punishment which is everlasting. One knows all the objections, most of them not very impressive because the real problem is not the existence of Hell but the existence of suffering in any form. But the reason for believing in Hell is again not that we can answer the objections but that we submit our intellect to Christ. He knew God's love better than any man. Yet he believed and taught that his Father would one day separate the sheep from the goats. In a way this is but a reflection of the dignity of man. Precisely because we are neither animals nor imbeciles, God will call us to account. Precisely because we are bearers of the image of God, what we do during the few years we spend in this life has a significance that is eternal.

Imitating Him

A second implication of the fact that for us to live is Christ is that he is the One we seek to imitate. At one level, he is the image of God, from whose life and work we can deduce what God is like. Nothing in the whole Christian revelation is more marvellous than that – in God, there is no un-Christlikeness at all. But at another level, Christ is the archetypal man – the model man – God's great statement of what being a man means in this sinful world.

When we begin to work this out in detail, the results are fascinating.

We find, for example, that Christ needed companionship. Of all men, he must have been the most self-sufficient. Yet the social element in his life is very pronounced. Why did he choose the Twelve? We might suggest all kinds of great reasons. But Mark puts it with remarkable simplicity: he ordained Twelve to be with him; simply *to be with him*. He shrank from loneliness and it was not the least of his sorrows in the final crisis of his life that even those who were closest to him forsook him. There is surely some comfort here for those of us who are today finding it difficult to cope with isolation.

Again, we find that this Christ who is our example sometimes found it difficult to keep going. That's how we often feel ourselves and it doesn't help when those outside our situation tell us to 'buck up' and show some faith and some courage. Counsellors of one kind or another too often give the impression that it is a sin not to find life easy. Now I believe that it is possible, with God's help, to be content whatever state we are in. But such contentment is often attained only after a long spiritual struggle. That's the way it was with

Christ. In the Garden of Gethsemane, faced with the terrible agony of Calvary, he is despondent and afraid. That gives us the right to be despondent and afraid sometimes and it is a right for which we are profoundly thankful.

But there is something stranger still. Christ, our example, was a controversial figure. The Cross wasn't simply the inevitable result of his being human or of his living when and where he did, or even of his being the Man that he was. He brought it on himself. He said the wrong things, speaking out fearlessly against hypocrisy, error and humbug and giving terrible offence to the establishment, not least the religious establishment. He also identified with the wrong people – those too uneducated and too powerless or too frightened to speak for themselves. The poor, the children, the hated Romans and the still more-hated tax-collectors, even those of dubious moral reputation – at one time or another he becomes the spokesman of all of these. If we are to be authentic disciples, we must walk the same road. The danger always exists, of course, that controversy will nourish egotism and even hatred. Yet we cannot avoid it. Even at the risk of being assimilated and at the risk of being compromised, we must get involved. The Church cannot have a low profile, anymore than Christ could. It must go at the world – the secular world and the ecclesiastical world – even if the impression it creates is that, like him, it has a demon.

But the most demanding thing of all remains to be said. The Christ whom we are trying to follow and trying to emulate made himself nothing. He became a nonentity. It was not what he was, but it was what he looked like, what he allowed men to think of him and how he allowed men to treat him. He obscured his deity beneath humanness and ordinariness and suffering and even death. He didn't look great or clever. He had none of the trappings of popularity. Instead, he was despised and contemptible: a no-person. That is a hard road. But for the Christian it is the only road: one on which we are willing to renounce our rights, to be misunderstood, to be damned with faint praise, to serve and yet to be deemed absurd failures by those we are trying to help.

I cannot close this part of our theme, without saying one thing more. What upheld Christ? What kept him going? A sense of duty, of course, and love for lost men and women. But there was something else – what the Epistle to the Hebrews calls 'The joy set before him'. That has become very unfashionable today. But Christ was not ashamed to derive strength and courage from the great prospect – the prospect of glory with the Father – which lay before him. Neither should *we* be ashamed of it. Our hearts should turn often to the place where we shall see God; and where he shall meticulously wash away all the tears from our eyes.

Preaching Him

Thirdly, *to live is Christ* means that it is Christ we preach: indeed, that we live to preach him. It was in this context of a concern with preaching that Paul penned this great statement. He was content in his imprisonment because, as a result of it, Christ was being made more widely known. The result of his sufferings had been the furtherance of evangelism.

There are just two things I would like to say on that.

First, Paul didn't mind who preached the gospel so long as it was being preached. He had had trouble in this connection. Some were preaching in a party spirit, trying to strengthen their own following. Other preachers, he knew, were envious of himself and of the way God had blessed him. Some were even trying to take his place in the affection of the believers at Philippi. The marvellous thing was that Paul didn't mind. The motives of these men were all wrong and they would answer to God for that. But the important thing was that they were preaching the truth. The message was right and that was what mattered. That must be our standard. It is of no consequence what denomination a man belongs to and of even less consequence what he happens to think of us. If he preaches the lordship and the risenness of Christ, and proclaims his power to save, we, with Paul, rejoice, yes and will rejoice.

Secondly, and this must be said, not only tenderly, but in the terrible knowledge that I, myself, am open to judgment — whoever preaches another gospel, let him be anathema; even, says Paul, though it be an angel from heaven. It may be a great New Testament scholar denying the resurrection of Christ; or a leading ecclesiastic denying the need for men to be born again, saying that all go to heaven anyway. Let him be anathema. It may be a Free Churchman placing our own brand of tradition over Holy Scripture. Let him be anathema. It may be me, given over by God to a reprobate mind and destroying the faith I am called to establish. Let me be anathema. Don't all of us who preach in today's climate of theological indifferentism need to take this urgently to heart? Better to be wrong in the motive and right in the message than wrong in the message and right in the motive.

Today, a great army of preachers – numbering several thousand – will descend on Scotland. What potential even in a day of declining Church attendances! And what a wasted opportunity, that so many, rather than make some attempt, however humble, to expose the meaning of Christ, will regale their congregations with political comment, amusing anecdote and lifeless moralism.

But I cannot close on that note. If for us to live is Christ, then declares Paul, to die is gain. What an extraordinary thing to say! But Paul meant it. He had a desire, a strong desire, to depart this life. Why? Not because of world weariness. He had learned to be content. It was again, Christ. For most of us, death is terrifying because it separates us irreparably from those we love. For Paul, it was different.

Christ was the One he loved above all else and above all others. Death would not separate him from Christ. It would bring him closer, infinitely closer. He would see Christ better, hear him better, understand him better, serve him better.

What effect will death have on the bond between us and the thing we love most? — What we might call, for all practical purposes, our god?

ENDNOTES

Chapter 2

1.C.F.D. Moule, 'The Manhood of Jesus in the New Testament' in S.W.Sykes and J.P.Clayton (eds.), *Christ, Faith and History* (Cambridge: Cambridge University Press,1972), p.103.

2.Cited in H.R.Mackintosh, *The Doctrine of the Person of Jesus Christ* (Edinburgh: T&T Clark, 2nd edition 1913), p.277. For a fuller, first-hand account of Irving's views see *The Collected Writings of Edward Irving* (London,1865), Vol. V, pp.114-257.

3.Cited in Mackintosh as above, p.277.

4.K.Barth, *Church Dogmatics I.2* (Edinburgh: T&T Clark,1956), p.152.

5.Barth, as above, p.153.

6.A.B.Bruce, *The Humiliation of Christ* (Edinburgh: T&T Clark, 1876), p.271.

7.Barth, *Church Dogmatics I.2*, p.182.

8.Barth, *Church Dogmatics IV.1* (Edinburgh: T&T Clark, 1956), pp.481, 484

9.M. Dods, *The Incarnation of the Eternal Word* (London, 1831), p.279.

Chapter 3

1.For Barth's treatment of the Temptations see *Church Dogmatics IV.1*, pp.259-273.

2.The full quotation, reflecting Bunyan's attitude as he lay in prison contemplating the gallows and yet far from sure of his own salvation, is as follows: "wherefore, thought I, the point being thus, I am for going on, and venturing my eternal state with Christ, whether I have comfort here or no; if God doth not come in, thought I, I will leap off the ladder even blindfold into eternity, sink or swim, come heaven, come hell; Lord Jesus, if thou wilt catch me, do; if not, I will venture for thy name." (Grace Abounding, 337. See *The Works of John Bunyan*, 1854 [r.i. Edinburgh, 1991], Vol. 1, p.49).

Chapter 4

1.O.Cullmann, *The Christology of the New Testament* (London: SCM Press, 2nd edition 1963), p.52.

2.A.Harnack, *What Is Christianity?* (London: 1904), p.147.

3.R.Bultmann, *Theology of the N ew Testament, Vol. 1* (London: SCM Press, 1952), p.33.

4.R.Bultmann, as above, p.3.

5.S.Cave, *The Person of Christ* (London: Duckworth, 1925), p.23.

6.J.Denney, *Jesus and the Gospel* (London: Hodder and Stoughton, 1908), p.234.

7.J.Denney, as above, p.365.

8.H.P.Liddon, *The Divinity of our Lord* (London: Longmans, Green & Co.,14th edition,1908), p.176.

Chapter 5

1. A.Moody-Stuart, *Recollections of the late John Duncan* (Edinburgh, 1872), p.105. Duncan was commenting on the words of Ps. 22.1, "My God, my God, why has thou forsaken me?": "ay, ay, d'ye know what it was, dying on the cross, forsaken by His Father – d'ye know what it was? What? What? It was damnation – and damnation taken lovingly."

Chapter 6

1. J.Moltmann, *The Crucified God* (London: SCM Press, 1974.

2. J.Moltmann, as above, p.51.

3. Cited in A Stewart and J K Cameron, *The Free Church of Scotland 1843-1910* (Edinburgh: William Hodge and Company, 1910), p.285.'

4. John Dick, *Lectures on Theology* (Edinburgh, 1838), Vol. 1, p.361.

Chapter 7

1. Luther, *Lectures on Galatians 1535*, commenting on Galatians 3:13.

The full statement is: "And all the prophets saw this, that Christ was to become the greatest thief, murderer, adulterer, robber, desecrator, blasphemer, etc. there has ever been any where in the world." Behind this language there lies a clear doctrine of substitution: "Whatever sins I, you and all of us have committed or may commit in the future, they are as much Christ's own as if

He Himself had committed them." See Luther's Works, Vol. 26 (Saint Louis: Concordia Publishing House, 1963), p.279. These sentiments did not appear in the 1519 edition of the Lectures on Galatians.

2.Anselm, *Cur Deus Homo?*, Bk I.XXI

3.D.M.Baillie, *God Was In Christ* (London: Faber, 1948), p.184

4.K.Barth, *Church Dogmatics IV.1*, p. 229.

5.H.Martin, *The Atonement* (London, 1870 [r.i.Edinburgh, 1976]), 146.

6.C.H.Dodd, *The Bible and the Greeks* (London: Hodder & Stoughton, 1933), pp. 82-95. See also C.H.Dodd, *The Epistle of Paul to the Romans* (London: Fontana, 1959), pp. 47-50.

7.L.Morris, *The Apostolic Preaching of the Cross* (London: Tyndale Press, 2nd edition 1960), pp. 125-185; R Nicole, *Standing Forth* (Fearn: Mentor, 2002), pp. 343-385 ("*C H Dodd and the Doctrine of Propititiation*")

8.The phrase is taken from The Westminster Confession of Faith, Chapter XX ("Of Christian Liberty and Liberty of Conscience").

9.See *Luther's Works, Vol. 31* (Philadelphia: Fortress Press, 1957), p. 374.

10.G.Aulen, *Christus Victor* (London: SPCK, 1965).

11.Thomas Crawford, *The Scripture Doctrine of the Atonement* (Edinburgh: Blackwood, 3rd edition 1880), p. 125.

12.H.Martin, *The Atonement,* p.250.

Chapter 8

1.W.Pannenberg, *Jesus: God and Man* (London: SCM Press, 1968), pp.74-87.

2.A.Moody-Stuart, *Recollections of the late John Duncan* (Edinburgh, 1872), p.186.

3.Calvin, *A Harmony of the Gospels of Matthew, Mark and Luke, Vol. III* (Carlisle: Paternoster Press, 1995), p.99.

Chapter 9

1.C.H.Dodd, *The Epistle of Paul to the Romans* (London: Fontana, 1959), p. 165.

2.J.Hick (Ed.), *The Myth of God Incarnate* (London: SCM Press, 1977), p.21. C Anderson Scott, *Christianity according to St Paul* (Cambridge: Cambridge University Press, 1966), p.273.

3.R.Bultmann, *Theology of the New Testament* (London: SCM Press, 1965), Vol. 1, p.129.

4.B.B.Warfield, *Textual Criticism of the New Testament* (London: Hodder & Stoughton, 1893), p.185.

5.F.F.Bruce, *Commentary on the Book of the Acts* (London: Marshall, Morgan & Scott, 1954), fn.59, p.416.

6.O.Cullmann, *The Christology of the New Testament* (London: SCM Press, 1963), p.312.

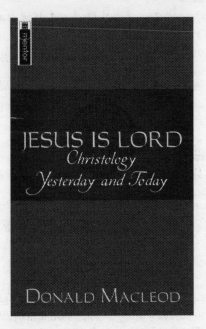

JESUS IS LORD
Christology
Yesterday and Today

DONALD MACLEOD

Jesus is Lord

Christology – Yesterday and Today

Donald Macleod

The Deity of Jesus has been questioned by many theologians. In this volume Donald Macleod, author of a much-acclaimed volume of Christology, considers the crucial evidences.

Macleod begins by examining three important descriptions from the New Testament itself – 'God over all', 'Jesus is Lord' and 'The Son of Man'.

He then surveys the influence of Arminianism, including the effect it had on the famous hymn writer Isaac Watts and on the well-known authors Philip Doddridge. This is followed with a chapter on the doctrine of the incarnation in Scottish Theology where he responds to such theologians as Donald Baillie, James Denney and T.F. Torrance.

The final two chapters consider the Christologies of Jurgen Moltmann and Wolfhart Pannenberg.

This is a book that should engage the mind of all thinking Christians. As Macleod says in the preface about the contents "Their common theme is Christ. Their common object is to explore and vindicate his glory'.

ISBN 1 85792 4851

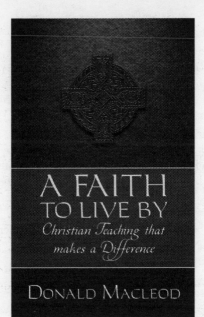

A FAITH
TO LIVE BY
Christian Teaching that
makes a Difference

DONALD MACLEOD

A Faith to Live By

Understanding Christian Doctrine

Donald Macleod

A comprehensive examination of Christian Doctrine, practically explained.

'Macleod is a master of making difficult things seem simple, without compromising their profundity…Macleod is simultaneously an able apologist and a world class exegete (one does not hesitate to mention his name alongside Warfield and Murray in exegetical competence). Read the book. Learn from Macleod. Argue with Macleod. And then bow the knee to your Saviour, the Lord Jesus Christ, and worship!'

**J. Ligon Duncan III,
First Presbyterian Church, Jackson, Mississippi**

"Macleod writes with lucid and sparkling clarity, without sacrifice of detail and definition. Here is excellent theology made both relevant and exciting. I can think of no better book for equipping Christians to present their faith intelligently and attractively to real people.'

John D. Nicholls, London City Mission

'I have always valued Donald Macleod's writings, his great learning, his respect for those with whom he disagrees, the absence of foolish dogmatism and the presence of a pastoral heart. Here we have first rate Christian theology, exceedingly encouraging for a Christian teacher who knows a lot, and marvellous illumination for the Christian neophyte who knows nothing, but wants to learn'.

Dick Lucas, The Proclamation Trust

ISBN 1 85792 4282

Behold Your God

Donald Macleod

'*This Study of God compels praise and service*'
Fergus Macdonald, United Bible Society

'*...evidences a rare combination of pastoral concerns, powerful doctrinal exposition, and searching application of truth*'
**J. Ligon Duncan III,
First Presbyterian Church, Jackson , Mississippi**

'*Donald Macleod brings the familiar to life with a freshness that is stimulating and delightful*'
John Nicholls, London City Mission

Looking at the attributes of God in easily accessible language, Donald Macleod leads us towards a greater understandingand a fresh discovery of the God of the Bible.

With a specifically Biblical approach, our focus is continually brought back to Christ - The supreme revelation of God. We are reminded that all the facets of God's character and nature are to be found in Christ, and each step of discovery is a constant challenge to us to respond appropriately to that earth- shattering reality.

ISBN 1 87167 6509

The Spirit of Promise

Donald Macleod

In recent years a great deal has been said and written regarding the person and work of the Holy Spirit. One result of this has been the alienation between so called Charismatics and the more traditional branches of the Christian Church.

This book deals with the issues which have led to the controversy and the author's viewpoint will no doubt provoke both positive and negative reactions. Whatever the reader's particular opinions there is much food for thought in each of the chapters.

As Professor Macleod says in the introduction, 'The questions they deal with are likely to be with us for some time.'

ISBN 0 906731 488

Rome and Canterbury

A View from Geneva

Donald Macleod

A thought provoking analysis of the ongoing discussion between the Roman Catholic Church and the Church of England.

In a courteous and clear way the issues are highlighted, with differing points of view acknowledged and dealt with.

If you are interested in developments within the Anglican and Roman Catholic Churches then this book will stimulate - and give you a clear grasp of the debate.

Topics covered include

The Place of Scripture
The Ordination of Women
The Holy Spirit and Church Infallibility
The Canon of Scripture

A penetrating examination by a brilliant theologian.

ISBN 0 906731 887

Shared Life

The Trinity and the
Fellowship of God's People

Donald Macleod

'...the simplicity of his style of communication will commend this book to all kinds of folk who currently would have problems in explaining their belief inthe Trinity. He commences with proof from Scripture, and adds to this evidence from early Church thnkers before applying Trinitarian religion in a practical way to ourselves... A sound book with the potential to be blessed to many.'

Christian Bookstore Journal

'...gives us a helpful look at the objections raised by Judaism, Islam, Mormonism and the Jehovah Witnesses... extremely helpful. Donald Macleod writes with his customary clarity.'

Evangelism

What is the Trinity?
Why does it matter?
How should it affect us?

'The Doctrine of the Trinity is not simply something to be believed, but something that ought to affect our lives profoundly', say Donald Macleod in this useful book that teaches us about the concept and implications of the doctrine of the Trinty

ISBN 1 85792 128 3

Christian Focus Publications publishes books for all ages.

Our mission statement –

STAYING FAITHFUL

In dependence upon God we seek to help make his infallible word, the Bible, relevant. Our aim is to ensure that the Lord Jesus Christ is presented as the only hope to obtain forgiveness of sin, live a useful life and look forward to heaven with him.

REACHING OUT

Christ's last command requires us to reach out to our world with his gospel. We seek to help fulfill that by publishing books that point people towards Jesus and for them to develop a Christ-like maturity. We aim to equip all levels of readers for life, work ministry and mission.

Books in our adult range are published in three imprints.

Christian Heritage contains classic writings from the past.
Mentor focuses on books written at a level suitable for Bible College and seminary students, pastors, and other serious readers; the imprint includes commentaries, doctrinal studies, examination of current issues, and church history.
Christian Focus contains popular works including biographies, commentaries, basic doctrine, and Christian living. Our children's books are also published in this imprint.

For a free catalogue of all our titles, please write to
Christian Focus Publications, Ltd
Geanies House, Fearn,
Ross-shire, IV20 1TW, Scotland, United Kingdom
info@christianfocus.com

For details of our titles visit us on our website
www.christianfocus.com